HOW TO PRAY

John Pritchard is Bishop of Oxford and was formerly Bishop of Jarrow. He was Archdeacon of Canterbury and, before that, Warden of Cranmer Hall, Durham. He has served in parishes in Birmingham and Taunton, and has been Diocesan Youth Officer for Bath and Wells diocese. Other books by the author include *The Intercessions Handbook*, *The Second Intercessions Handbook*, *Beginning Again*, *Living Easter Through the Year*, *How to Explain Your Faith*, *The Life and Work of a Priest* and *Going to Church: A user's guide*. He is married to Wendy and has two married daughters.

HOW TO PRAY

A PRACTICAL HANDBOOK

John Pritchard

First published in Great Britain in 2002

Society for Promoting Christian Knowledge
36 Causton Street
London SW1P 4ST

British Library Cataloguing-in-Publication Data
A catalogue record for this book is available from the
British Library

ISBN 978-0-281-05454-1

10 9 8 7 6

Typeset by Wilmaset Ltd, Birkenhead, Wirral
First printed in Great Britain by
The Cromwell Press, Trowbridge, Wiltshire
Reprinted in Great Britain by Ashford Colour Press

Produced on paper from sustainable forests

For colleagues and friends in the dioceses of Canterbury and Durham.

CONTENTS

FOREWORD ix
ACKNOWLEDGEMENTS xi
A WORD OF INTRODUCTION xiii

PART ONE: WATCH THIS SPACE

1 How to make the first moves 3
2 How to slow down 5
3 How to start saying something 8
4 How to listen to the silent music 11
5 How to keep your feet on the ground 14

Markers on the way: 1 The model prayer 17

PART TWO: DAY BY DAY

6 How to start the day with God 23
7 How to pray through the day 25
8 How to use a special time of prayer 29
9 How to pray for other people 32
10 How to end the day with God 36

Markers on the way: 2 Prayer and action 40

PART THREE: GOOD PRACTICE

11 How to pray with the Bible 45
12 How to pray with the Gospels – the Ignatian way 48
13 How to pray with the community – the Benedictine way 51
14 How to pray with the emotions – the Franciscan way 55
15 How to pray with everyday life – the Celtic way 59

Markers on the way: 3 A rule of life 62

PART FOUR: PRAYING WITH ALL WE'VE GOT

16 How to pray with the imagination 67
17 How to soak in silence 70
18 How to enter the mystery 73
19 How to use music and the arts 76
20 How to pray in church 79

Markers on the way: 4 Sacred times and sacred places 83

PART FIVE: DARKNESS AND LIGHT

21 How to pray in bad times 89
22 How to pray in the wilderness 91
23 How to think through problems 95
24 How to stay fresh 98
25 How to make all of life a prayer 100

Markers on the way: 5 Setting the compass 103

RESOURCES 107

FOREWORD

A book about prayer whose author is up-front enough to admit that 'sometimes, prayer is simply boring', just *has* to be taken seriously! But the reader who ventures within the pages of John Pritchard's excellent book will certainly be far from bored.

How to Pray positively encourages a reckless profligacy with adjectives. Approachable, down-to-earth, refreshing, informative, humorous and moving – these are only some of the words clamouring to be used of a book that represents a major contribution in an area that can be as difficult as it is hugely important.

Totally devoid of even the faintest whiff of condescension, this book reaches out to meet with people where they really are. It celebrates the blessed accessibility of a God who is 'open all hours' and who, in His patient longing, is content simply to 'hang about': a God in whose gentle converse the profane is hallowed, the secular is made sacred and our whole world is transfigured.

David Hope

ACKNOWLEDGEMENTS

Biblical quotations are taken from the New Revised Standard Version of the Bible, copyright © 1989 by the Division of Christian Education of the National Council of the Churches of Christ in the USA. Used by permission. All rights reserved.

The author and publisher acknowledge with thanks permission to reproduce the following material:

p.61, adapted from David Adam, 'A Celtic prayer', *The Open Gate*, Triangle, 1994.

pp.75–6, D. H. Lawrence, 'Pax', *The Complete Poems of D. H. Lawrence*, eds Vivian de Sola Pinto and F. Warren Roberts, Penguin, 1964. Used by permission of Laurence Pollinger Ltd and the Estate of Frieda Lawrence Ravagli.

p.76, Michel Quoist, 'Before You, Lord', *Prayers for Life*, Gill and Macmillan, 1963.

p.91, Timothy Rees, 'God is Love', *Hymns Ancient and Modern*, No 365, Canterbury Press, 1950, 1996.

p.102, Rex Chapman, from 'The Glory of God'.

Other extracts are from the following sources:

p.4, G. K. Chesterton, *Autobiography*, Burns and Oates, 1937.

p.5, John Drane, 'Dunblane: A Personal Testimony', *The Search for Faith and Witness of the Church*, Church House Publishing, 1996.

p.8, Toki Miyashina, in *The Lion Book of Famous Prayers*, Lion, 1983.

p.13, G. B. Shaw, *Saint Joan*, Penguin, 2001.

p.16, Kenneth Leech, *True Prayer*, Sheldon Press, 1980.

p.25, Iona, adapted from *A Wee Worship Book*, Wild Goose Publications, 1999.

p.27–8, Brother Lawrence, *The Practice of the Presence of God*, Hodder and Stoughton, 1989.

p.28, Lord Astley, in *Pocket Prayers*, ed. Christopher Herbert, National Society/Church House Publishing, 1994.

pp.31–2, St Augustine, *Confessions*, Penguin, 1961.

pp.35–6, Anthony Bloom, *School for Prayer*, DLT, 1970.

p.39, Richard of Chichester, in *Pocket Prayers*, ed. Christopher Herbert, National Society/Church House Publishing, 1994.

pp.41–2, Kenneth Leech, *True Prayer*, Sheldon Press, 1980.

p.42, Anglican Church of the Province of New Zealand, New Zealand Prayer Book, HarperCollins, 1997.

p.42, Martin Luther King, 'A blessing', in *The Lion Book of Famous Prayers*, Lion, 1983.

p.47, Martin L. Smith, *The Word is Very Near You: A Guide to Praying with Scripture*, Cowley Publications, 1989.

pp.47–8, Collect for the last Sunday after Trinity, *Common Worship*, Church House Publishing, 2000.

p.57, Fyodor Dostoevsky, *The Brothers Karamazov*, Penguin, 1993.

p.57, Papas Fynn, *Mister God, This is Anna*, Ballantine, 2000.

p.58, Francis of Assisi, *Canticle of the Sun*, traditional.

p.72, Michael Stancliffe, *Stars and Angels*, Canterbury Press, 1997.

p.80, Annie Dillard, *Pilgrim at Tinker's Creek*, Perennial, 1998.

p.84, St Augustine, *Confessions*, Penguin, 1961.

p.89, Carol Bialock, in Sheila Cassidy, *Good Friday People*, DLT, 1991.

p.90–1, Khalil Gibran, *The Prophet*, Heinemann, 1980.

p.92, Henri Nouwen, *Sabbatical Journey*, Crossroad, 1998.

p.94, Anthony Bloom, *Living Prayer*, DLT, 1966.

p.101, C. S. Lewis, *Mere Christianity*, Fount, 1997.

p.101, Julian of Norwich, *Revelations of Divine Love*, Penguin, 1966.

The author and publisher would also like to thank the following for permission to use their drawings and cartoons:

Paul Judson, on pp.17, 40, 62, 83 and 103

The Revd Ron Wood, on pp.xiii, 28, 32, 35, 54, 78 and 82

Every effort has been made to acknowledge fully the material quoted in this book, and to contact the copyright holders. We apologize for any omissions and would ask those concerned to contact the publisher, who will ensure that full acknowledgement is made in the future.

A WORD OF INTRODUCTION

Surveys consistently show that we pray more than we like to admit. It seems in many ways that we're more aware of our spiritual nature than ever, but we go searching for the right clothes to wear for this part of our lives in many strange boutiques! An article in a lifestyle magazine encouraged its readers to be spiritual because it lowers stress and blood pressure, boosts your immune system, fights depression, makes you more efficient and it's 'never been so sexy'. The article suggested trying Buddhism, yoga, feng shui, crystals, aromatherapy, shiatsu and shamanism. But the only mention Christianity got was because the singer Madonna was supposed to have given it up!

My belief, however, is that not only is there life yet in the old dog of Christianity, but there's also a deep and compelling instinct to pray which other fashionable forms of spirituality can't meet. Years ago St Augustine caught the truth precisely. One of his prayers starts: 'Almighty God, you have made us for yourself, and our hearts are restless till they find their rest in you ...' If that's true, if our lives cannot be fulfilled outside a relationship with the beauty and mystery we call God, then prayer becomes not a religious bolt-on to a 'pretty-good' life, but an essential ingredient of being fully human.

Many people are plagued with the fear of an unlived life – a scattered

The Revd Habakkuk Wilkins was the victim of a bizarre meditation accident.

existence of secondary things. We recognize the danger that while we're
becoming amazingly proficient in new
technologies, the human heart is in
danger of shrinking, or at the very
least that we're not coping well with
the huge waves of cultural change which
are pouring over us. But we also don't
want the depressing moralism and ob-
session with structures which seems to
be all that's left of some conventional
religion. And we know that we need
something pretty big and substantial to
meet our need. As one writer put it:
'You can't rely on candy floss to fix
malnutrition.'

So maybe it *is* the living God we need
after all. Maybe it's the breathtaking,
alpine beauty of the Creator. Maybe we
need to respond to the tug of that slow,
steady undertow of longing that we
sense sometimes when we slow down
enough. Maybe prayer is the hidden
wiring of human life that connects us to
the world wide web of the Spirit.
Maybe prayer is exhilarating and
stretching and healing, and open to
humour and anger and joy beyond
imagining.

Maybe. And that's what this book is
all about.

PART ONE: WATCH THIS SPACE

I HOW TO MAKE THE FIRST MOVES

It happens to most of us at some time or other. A faint stirring somewhere that there may be more to this life than meets the eye? The thought just flits across our air-space – 'I wonder ... is there something else?' Perhaps something really brilliant or really tragic happens, and we're not sure what to do with it. Perhaps we meet someone who really impresses us and we discover that person is a Christian. Or we go into a cathedral and something gently tugs at our subconscious. Maybe it even gets as far as a sense of reaching out from inside ourselves for something. But what? That elusive 'something else'.

Or maybe it even gets as far as a sense of gratitude, a sense of something given. 'Thank God for that,' we say, before we realize what we've said. Because God for many of us is still very much an open question. So it's really rather embarrassing to feel gratitude when we're not sure who to thank. But we fall crazily in love with a person or a place or simply with life itself, and we reach instinctively for someone to thank.

All of these are common human experiences, but we usually don't notice them and they get buried under an avalanche of new experiences surging along behind. These stirrings, however, may be profoundly significant. This tentative 'reaching out' may be like a fragile plant pushing its way through concrete, but it may be the first playful sign of a huge spiritual adventure.

One writer talked about 'signals of transcendence' which litter our everyday experience. And indeed there are things going on all the time, like longing, laughter, falling in love, playing with a child, natural beauty ('breathtaking'), moments in music ('heart-stopping') – all of which take us outside ourselves for a moment. There's something else going on here. I wonder ...?

So the first move in the spiritual adventure that I'm here calling 'prayer' is to recognize these moments when something stirs within us and to savour them. Not to let them be flooded and forgotten, but to notice them and hold them, tenderly, just for a while. And for the time being – that's enough! Just recognize those moments for what they are, or might be. Signals of something else. A hint of something good. A glimpse in the night. A scent on the wind. An invitation.

There's nothing pushy or invasive about these stirrings. They're gentle, quiet, courteous even. But then maybe that's God's way. After all, Christians say he crept in through the back door of human history in that child in a dirty stable in an occupied land. Nothing aggressive or demanding there. Just an invitation to live life to the full.

I wonder?

A different approach

Another way we get alerted to the possibility of 'something else' is when we're in trouble. It may be illness or an accident either to us or someone we care about. It may be a serious job interview or a fear of flying. Or it may simply be that there are no atheists in the exam room! But for whatever reason, we may find ourselves, almost against our wishes, appealing to God, fate or the Great Pattern in the Sky. Many a bargain is struck in the recesses of the heart when things look black, only to be discarded with embarrassment when the good times return. But it may still be a reminder that none of us is self-sufficient; we all face situations when we know we could do with someone big on our side. We may dismiss it as childish later on, but we can't deny the power of the instinct to reach out beyond ourselves. And reaching out beyond ourselves is the first move in prayer.

KEY QUESTION

When has something stopped you, stirred you, made you ask a deeper question? And how would you describe that experience – good? odd? disturbing? reassuring? Or what?

TRY THIS

- Try to notice these 'something else' moments when they occur during this week. Hold them gently, there and then, if you can. And remember them, put them in your pocket, and bring them out in a quieter moment to think more about them and what they might mean for you.
- Try to pay a bit more attention to what's going on *inside* you rather than to outer events and activities. Listen to your moods and feelings and don't just brush them aside if they're different or strange. Listen to those moods. Our inner life is as full and rich as our outer life; it's just that we usually don't notice.

QUOTES

At the back of our brains there is a forgotten blaze or burst of astonishment at our own existence. The object of the artistic and spiritual life is to dig for this sunrise of wonder.
G. K. Chesterton

Although I'm an agnostic, I sometimes pray, but I don't ask for anything, except sometimes the ability to get through something. Usually – this sounds unbearably pious – I give thanks.
John Diamond, a journalist who was living with cancer

STORY

At Dunblane after the murder of 16 school children and their teacher in 1996:
I made my way to the school gates. As I approached, the street outside the school was deserted apart from a handful of police officers and a gang of youths aged about 17–20. As I watched, they took from their pockets 16 nightlights and, kneeling on the damp pavement, arranged them in a circle and then lit them. They stood around the candles for a moment, then one of them said, 'I suppose someone should say something.' As they wondered how to do it, one of them spotted me, identified me as a minister, and called me over with the words 'You'll know what to say.' Of course the reality was quite different. As I stood there, tears streaming down my face, I had no idea what to say or how to say it. So we stood, holding on to one another for a moment, and then I said a brief prayer. That was the catalyst. A question came first: 'What kind of world is this?' Another asked, 'Is there any hope?' Someone said, 'I wish I could trust God.' 'I'll need to change,' said a fourth one. As he did so he glanced over his shoulder to the police. He reached into his pocket and I could see he had a knife. He knelt by the ring of candles and quietly said, 'I'll not be needing this now', as he tucked it away under some of the flowers lying nearby. One of the others produced a piece of bicycle chain and did the same. We stood silently for a moment, and then went our separate ways.

John Drane

2 HOW TO SLOW DOWN

So there just might be something in it – this 'something else'. And we might have noticed some germ of an instinct, some stirring inside. A reaching out. An instinct to say thank you, a need to say sorry, or a desire to help someone. But we can all too easily lose the moment unless we make space for it to breathe.

And that's what we're terribly short of in our culture – space to let quiet things breathe. The pace of daily life is accelerating and the demands are unremitting. It's as if we got on the 8.15 from Great Snoring, the slow train that stops at every little village, but instead of chugging its way gently through the countryside it gets faster and faster, accelerating steadily and inexorably, streaming through every station, until the carriage is swaying alarmingly and we're hanging on to our seats and to our luggage – and still the speed increases! When is it going to come off the tracks?

Or here's another image. You know when your suitcase is full, and not just full, but absolutely full to bursting? You jam another shirt in and kneel on the case to shut it. And now there's a sweater you'd forgotten. You stand on the case to force it shut. No more, you say! And then you realize you've left out your sponge bag. It's just no use. You can't fit anything else in. You need a different strategy. You need to start again.

In a culture where speed and the ability to 'pack more in' is becoming self-defeating, many people are crying out for space. They long to slow down. A group of porters were once rushing through the jungle at a ridiculous pace set by the Europeans who had hired them. Eventually they got to a clearing and sat down. The Europeans tried to get them moving again but the head porter said, 'No, we're not moving. We've come so far and so fast that now we have to wait for our souls to catch up with us.' So does our culture.

Individually, therefore, we need to build some slowing-down time into our lives. Then we can listen to the quiet whispers from another country that we're just becoming aware of. We need to look for the moments of calm in our day and stretch them out. We need to create times for stopping, taking everything out of the case and trying a different way of packing altogether. Slowing down is a vital part of the spiritual journey. Then we can stop panicking about when we're going to come off the rails, and start noticing the fascinating countryside we're travelling through.

Imagine a glass of muddy water. When it's shaken up and disturbed the water becomes murky and unpleasant. Let the glass rest, however, and you see the cloudiness in the water gradually clear as the dirt settles to the bottom. Eventually you have clear water and a dark sediment beneath. In some such way, when we slow down, the water of our inner life clears and we're able to see and understand what's really going on inside us. This is the next stage of our spiritual journey.

KEY QUESTION

When are the potential 'slow-down' times in your day? Don't pretend there aren't any! It might only be in the bathroom or in bed at night, but equally it might be walking the dog, driving, waiting at a checkout, or a dozen other times. So when are they – for you?

TRY THIS

- Before you start a new piece of work (home-work, house-work, office-work) pause for a moment before you get into it. Reflect on how you feel about what you've just finished and what you are about to do. Are you feeling OK? Is it something to give thanks for, or to ask for help with? Or do you just need to stop and enjoy a moment of simply being yourself?

- When you walk from one place to another, try walking more slowly. It may be difficult to slow your normal pace, so be deliberate in slowing down. Breathe more gently, be aware of your body as you move, notice what's around you. And, as they say – enjoy!

- Make an appointment with yourself. The psychologist Carl Jung was asked by a client for an appointment at a particular time and he looked in his diary and said he couldn't make it because he already had an appointment then. When the first time came, the client was in a boat and saw Jung by the lakeside, by himself, with his feet in the water, doing nothing. When their new appointment came, the client expressed his annoyance with Jung that he had actually been doing nothing at the time he'd asked for. 'Not at all,' said Jung, 'an appointment with myself is one I never break.' Do the same. Promise yourself some space to do anything or nothing. Slow down. Stop. You may find Someone Special waiting to meet you.

QUOTE

Love has its speed. It is an inner speed. It is a spiritual speed. It is a different kind of speed from the technological speed to which we are accustomed. It goes on in the depths of our life, whether we notice or not, at three miles an hour. It is the speed we walk and therefore it is the speed the love of God walks.

Kosuke Koyama

STORY

A man went to see a monk with a reputation for spiritual wisdom. He asked the monk to teach him about the spiritual journey, and proceeded to talk non-stop about himself and all his ideas. Eventually the monk got up and made a cup of tea, while the man kept on talking. The monk started pouring the tea into his visitor's cup but when it was full he still carried on pouring. The tea went over into the saucer and still the monk went on pouring. It spilled over the saucer and on to the table – and still he went on pouring. At last the visitor could restrain himself no longer. 'Don't you see,' he said, 'the cup is already full!' 'Exactly,' said the monk. 'And so are you. You're so full of yourself and your own ideas there's no room for me to teach you anything.'

An image: the top floor

Imagine your life represented by a house. The ground floor is the area you're prepared for others to see and share. They come into your kitchen and living room and you entertain and enjoy them. Upstairs are your own more private rooms, the bedroom and bathroom. These aren't public rooms; they're for your rest and revitalization, and also for intimacy with those you love. But up on the top floor is your own study or workplace, far away from the noise and clatter of downstairs. This is where you are most truly yourself with your own thoughts and dreams, your plans and promises. It's where you sit quietly and enjoy the calm. This is the place you need to return to, often enough to keep in touch with your real self and to stay on course.

PSALM 23 FOR BUSY PEOPLE

The Lord is my Pace-Setter, I shall not rush,
He makes me stop and rest for quiet
*   intervals,*
He provides me with images of stillness,
*   which restore my serenity.*

He leads me in ways of efficiency, through
*   calmness of mind; and his guidance is*
*   peace.*
Even though I have a great many things to
*   accomplish each day, I will not fret, for*
*   his presence is here.*
His timelessness, his all-importance will
*   keep me in balance.*
He prepares refreshment and renewal in
*   the midst of my activity, by anointing my*
*   mind with his oils of tranquillity,*
My cup of joyous energy overflows.
Surely harmony and effectiveness shall be
*   the fruits of my hours,*
For I shall walk in the pace of my Lord, and
*   dwell in his house for ever.*
*   Toki Miyashina*

3 HOW TO START SAYING SOMETHING

When we've noticed that there may be 'something else' going on in our lives, and then tried to make some space to stretch out those experiences a bit, there'll come a time when we'll probably want to use words in what we might begin to call 'prayer'.

Words aren't compulsory! It's just that we're speaking animals and we've always entrusted our thoughts and feelings to words in a desire to communicate with each other – and with God. And one of the big truths shared by Christianity, Judaism and Islam is that God is talkative; he too seems to have wanted to communicate with us through words. Christians in particular have wanted to use spoken words, to be faithful to the written word, to lead us to the living Word – Jesus himself.

Of course, we live in a society that uses words in vast quantities. We send them everywhere, by letter, fax, e-mail, inter-net, phone, junk mail, a huge output of newspapers and magazines. We're drowning in words, but rarely is there much judgement or discernment about our use of them. We're simply promis-cuous with them. T. S. Eliot wrote of 'the slimy mud of words, the sleet and hail of verbal imprecision'.

And yet words are the best tools we've got for communication, so it shouldn't be surprising that our venture into prayer will soon take us into this dangerous arena. We've slowed down in order to give opportunity for those stirrings of thankfulness, wonder or need to see the light of day. We've made space to get in touch with what's going on inside us. Now comes the desire to speak to the 'something else' that seems increasingly like a Someone Else.

But what shall we say?

THREE THINGS THAT DON'T MATTER

1 **Quantity.** We don't have to say a lot. We just have to say what we want, or what we feel strongly about. In any case, saying a lot may mean we lose the point. Woody Allen once said, 'I took a speed reading course and read *War and Peace* in twenty minutes. It's about Russia.' Prayer is about life, all of it, but we don't need to talk about it all at once!

2 **Quality.** We don't have to speak well, in good English, with nicely rounded phrases. Authenticity is what matters. It's a conversation, not an exam.

3 **Knowledge.** We don't need to have a theology degree to speak to God any more than we need a medical degree to speak to a doctor. Prayer is for amateurs, and we remain amateurs all our lives.

TWO THINGS THAT DO MATTER

1 **Being natural.** In the Bible it's said that Moses talked with God 'as with a friend' (Exodus 33.11). That's the model. We simply talk with him about anything and everything, in the sporadic, or focused, or 'um-er' way we talk to anyone in the daily round of our lives. When we talk to God there's no need to put on evening dress.

2 **Being honest.** A schoolboy was very angry about his parents splitting up, and that anger spilled over on to God. He heard a sermon about Jacob arguing and fighting with God through the night, so he went back to his room and burst out, 'God, I hate you.' 'Excellent,' said his chap-lain, later. Why? Because he was being honest. The psalms are full of the passionate cries of honest people venting their feelings before God. Honesty is what God deals with best.

TRY THIS

• When you notice during the day that you're feeling good about something, just say it to God, in whatever words come naturally. Similarly when there's something you feel worried about, like an appointment or an interview. Or when you get news about someone you care about. Don't just feel it – say it. It's like talking to yourself, which we actually do much of the time; you just turn the talk outwards to God.

- If you want to say something in one of your 'slowing down' times when you have a real bit of space, you might like to put some order or shape into your prayer. One simple way is to take the route *Thank you, Sorry, Please.* It needn't take long, but this way you've covered some important ground of thanking God for whatever strikes you as good (the warmth of the sun, that special relationship, that friend's encouragement), of apologizing for wherever you've fouled up (be honest!) and of asking for the things that are on your heart for yourself and for others.
- If you feel a bit unsure about an undiluted diet of your own prayers, there are some very good books of prayers which you could use as part of your time of quiet. Ruth Etchells' *Just As I Am* often says beautifully what you wanted to say, as do any of the books by Eddie Askew and published by The Leprosy Mission. There are lots of books like this and it's good to look out for the unusual ones that will speak just your kind of language. Among resource books of prayers, Angela Ashwin's *Book of a Thousand Prayers* is obviously a big one, but excellent. A smaller book is

Pocket Prayers, compiled by Christopher Herbert and full of classic prayers which have stood the test of time.

JOKE BOX

An older lady had just gone to live in a warden-controlled flat. On her first morning the warden called up the old lady on the intercom to check if she was all right. 'Edith, Edith,' came the voice over the intercom. There was a pause, and then a frail voice replied: 'Speak, Lord, for thy servant heareth.'

THE SONG OF THE BIRD

The followers of the holy man were full of questions about God. The holy man said: 'God is the Unknown and the Unknowable. Every statement about him, every answer to your questions, is a distortion of the truth.'

The followers were bewildered. 'Then why do you speak about him at all?' they asked.

'Why does the bird sing?' said the holy man.

After Anthony de Mello

Sometimes we have to sing; sometimes we have to pray; sometimes we have to use words.

4 HOW TO LISTEN TO THE SILENT MUSIC

Prayer is sometimes spoken of as talking with God. But if that's the case, how come we hear so little from God's side? Perhaps we're gaining confidence that we can say things to God, however hesitantly, but the other end of the line seems pretty quiet. And in any case, if people say they hear the voice of God, we tend automatically to wonder about their medical history. So what does 'listening' mean in the context of prayer? And not in a way that requires a PhD in prayer – we're happy to be learning the alphabet here. What does listening to God mean for the beginner or the 'beginner-again'?

Essentially it means being open and attentive to God, who will be wanting to communicate his love to us in many more ways than simply with words. 'Listening' is a bit misleading. Words, or the faculty of hearing, are too narrow as categories. God communicates his presence to us through the whole fabric of life, but nearly always shyly, without attempting to overwhelm us and take away our freedom. God is always coming towards us, at every moment, and in everything that happens. Our task is to be more attentive to his coming, to listen between the lines, to catch the silent music.

Prayer, then, is simply being present to the presence of God, which we can do in a multitude of ways in the midst of life as well as when we give him time and priority. Prayer is being with God, in all sorts of ways and at all sorts of times. And when we're there, so is God. He may be there obviously or very quietly. We may be struck between the eyes or quite unaware of his presence. But he will always be there, gracefully active in the deep places of our lives. And we may become aware of this at any time – when we're putting out the washing, queuing in the supermarket, or listening to a colleague in a meeting. Be attentive – listen – and there'll be something deeper to discover. He may be hidden, but he's not hiding.

It was Woody Allen (again!) who said, 'Eighty per cent of life is just turning up.' So is prayer. Most of it is just turning up and letting God be God. If we're aware of him – great. If we're not – fine. He's still at work with us. He's got plenty of time, and he's a wonderful opportunist! Whatever we give him, he's always saying, 'Now what shall we make of this?'

But let's be particular. 'Listening' isn't about hearing voices; it's a much bigger attentiveness to a God who is always coming towards us at every moment. God always starts the conversation because he's always reaching out to us. But how will we notice his presence?

- Sometimes we might be aware of 'deep thoughts' – ideas and convictions which formulate themselves as we pause and pray. Listen to them, because they've at last been able to surface, and God may be in them. If so, they will have their own authenticity. We'll recognize their truth.
- Sometimes that moment of recognition will come through what others say, or what we read or see, or through events themselves, and we'll recognize the force of that insight as being for us. It drives home. It has the ring of truth about it. It may not strike anyone else; it's a personal 'disclosure'. It's God dealing with our heart.
- God often speaks to people through the language of creation. His world is just so stunningly beautiful, in the smallest detail or in the grandest sweep. Grown men are brought to tears by sunset in the Himalayas or left speechless by the incredible colours of the fish in the Gulf of Aqaba. Nature constantly amazes us and invites us to respond.
- Very often God will communicate through his special Word, the Bible. Here is the wisdom of God, actively seeking us out. In the interaction between this Book of Books and the deep places of our hearts God communicates through the electric charge of the Spirit. Sometimes we'll

be stopped in our tracks; sometimes we'll be challenged to the core; sometimes we'll be made aware of his incredible love. Our task is to listen to our hearts as we read the transcript of God's love.

- Another form of encounter with this God who is constantly coming towards us is through what may be a deep emotional response to music, or poetry, or a book or film, or someone relating an incident in their lives. From deep within comes a profound set of unexpected emotions with the divine signature discreetly upon them.

KEY QUESTION

Are you prepared to give God a chance to 'speak'? Will you practise 'pricking up your ears' to be open to his silent music in yourself, in others, in nature, in the Bible?

TRY THIS

- As you prepare for the day, determine to go into it with an open heart and mind. Be inquisitive not just to see what happens but what's happening under the surface. Be determined when you talk to someone, or go to a meeting, that you're not just going to read the surface events but you're going to listen to the deep language going on underneath. Listen for the truth.
- At the end of the day think about any particular event or experience you've

had that has been different and been painted in your mind in more vivid colours. It may have been a good experience, or uncomfortable, or full of humour, or deeply serious. Now as you ponder that event, what do you 'hear' in it, what do you draw out of it? What has that got to say to your own beliefs or values or ways of looking at things? What's the message for you?

- Try a short passage from the New Testament. Start by going bit by bit through Mark's Gospel or the letter to the Philippians. Read it carefully and slowly. Ponder it. Ask the questions: what was going on there? What does that say to me? What might I do about it? Then do the same tomorrow. Make a habit of it!

QUOTE

In Bernard Shaw's *Saint Joan,* after the coronation at Rheims, Joan pleads with the King and the Archbishop to continue the fight against the English because her 'voices' had ordered it. But the King is dismissive: 'O your voices, your voices,' he shouts. 'Why don't the voices come to me? I am the King, not you!'

And Joan replies, 'They do come to you, but you do not hear them. You have not sat in the field in the evening listening for them. When the Angelus rings you cross yourself and have done with it; but if you prayed from your heart and listened to the thrilling of the bells in the air after they stop ringing, you would hear the voices as well as I do.'

STORY

A man once wanted to find out about jade. He had a friend at work who said he knew an expert and could introduce him to him. The introduction was made and the man went along for his first lesson about jade.

He was shown into a room and the expert gave him a piece of jade and then left him, without explanation. So the man looked at his piece of jade, felt it, thought about it, but the expert didn't come back. Half an hour later he re-emerged and said the lesson was over and he would see him next week. The man was a bit mystified but he turned up next week and the same thing happened! He was shown into a room, given a piece of jade and left. Half an hour later the expert returned and said the lesson was over.

Each time the man went back the same thing happened and he was getting very cross. He was throwing good money after bad. Eventually he went to his friend at work, the one who had introduced him to the expert, and told him what he thought of these so-called lessons. 'All he does is hand me a piece of jade and then he disappears,' he complained. 'And blow me,' he went on, 'last week he had the cheek to give me a fake!'

Listen to the silent music.

5 HOW TO KEEP YOUR FEET ON THE GROUND

One of the fears we may have about this business of prayer is that it'll make us into spiritual nerds. I want to argue here that prayer isn't a super-spiritual technique for 'holy floaters' who move through life six inches off the ground and have a permanently pale and slightly pained expression on their faces. There's no need for an A level in holiness.

We have to recognize, nevertheless, that for some people their spirituality seems to loosen their grip on common sense. An American book of nursery rhymes for the Christian child offered this little masterpiece:

> Jack and Jill went up the hill,
> to fetch some Living Water.
> Drank it down and said they'd found
> joy and life ever after.

It doesn't even scan! Moreover, for others the life of prayer seems to be a rarified game of spiritual Monopoly, trying to gain the upper hand with a portfolio of the most valuable spiritual techniques. All this is to completely miss the point.

Prayer is essentially practical. It should make us more human, not less. It should give us resources to live our lives more fully, and to be more deeply engaged with others and with our communities. One Christian of the early Church said that 'the glory of God is a human being who is fully alive'. So let's not see prayer as something that draws us away from real life. It's precisely the opposite – it should make us enter the everyday realities of life more deeply.

I was once talking to a group of Christians on an inner-city estate. They were talking about how God could sometimes break through the spiritual wilderness of their community. One man put it rather colourfully: 'It's amazing how one little blade of grass can b***er up six inches of concrete,' he said. This was down-to-earth spirituality, reflecting vividly on what he saw God doing around him!

- Prayer is practical and down to earth. It leads into life, not away from it.
- Prayer is human and honest. It's not afraid of anger, frustration, tiredness and failure, nor of pleasure, passion, delight and success.
- Prayer is a healthy balance that engages the head, the heart and the hands. We should pray intelligently, with our feelings, and with the intention of doing something practical in response.
- Prayer is open to all, not just the

favoured few who happen to like that kind of thing. It's our birthright as Christians, and an extraordinary privilege too. But the other side of the coin is that an instant 'microwave' spirituality won't get us very far. Holiness is hard work.

KEY QUESTION

In what way has your experience of faith (however thick or thin that is) made you more fully human, more fully alive and more deeply engaged with the realities of life? If it hasn't, what's gone wrong?

A mapping exercise

Prayer is about exploring a relationship with God, not about perfecting an esoteric technique. It may help, therefore, to use an image of prayer like another deep relationship – that between husband and wife. If a marriage is to be healthy the relationship needs to exist at four levels:

1 **'Just getting on with it'**. Much of marriage is lived naturally and un-selfconsciously. We don't go on about it; we just live with that relationship as a backdrop. Similarly much of our relationship with God involves simply getting on with the pleasures and problems of living, but doing that against the background of God's good presence. And all of us can grin at God occasionally!

2 **Chatting**. An essential part of marriage is the daily sharing of a hundred minor conversations about nothing much at all. 'Do remember that dental appointment, won't you.' 'Could you get to the bank for me today?' 'I thought you were going to change that Damien Hirst poster in the kitchen?' Similarly, much of our day-to-day communication with God will be by chatting – what we call 'arrow prayers', i.e. quick-contact, instant-access prayers.

3 **Talking**. Any marriage needs proper conversation that gets down to things that matter. There may not be a lot of time in any one day, but thoughts, feelings, deeper things, need to come out and be shared. So with God. We need at some time to have the space and the focus of simply being with God, to deepen the relationship. This is where the going gets tough!

4 **Intimacy**. Marriage partners need to remain 'in touch' with each other – literally. They need to go beyond words to actions and the world of the senses. This is where touch, love and intimate silence have their place. In prayer too there is a time when words fall away and silence, meditation and the simple enjoyment of God take over.

TRY THIS (TO KEEP YOUR FEET ON THE GROUND)

- Use the checklist above on levels of relationship and apply it to your relationship with God. Do you want to adjust your own way of praying in any way yet? Or will you just keep this checklist in mind for future use?

- In an earlier age people used to say 'to work is to pray', *'laborare est orare'.* Try to see your daily activity as done for God. Offer it to him as the best you can do, and, if you can, see it as part of the hugely complex task God has of sustaining the world and making it better.

- When you come to a problem during the day ask yourself two questions: first, where is God in all this? Second, what's the Christ-like thing for me to do here? Those questions won't come naturally at first but if you train yourself to use them, they'll be a great resource at crucial moments.

- Try to use everyday events as material for prayer. When you watch the news or read the paper, refer the issues and crises straight to God. The same with the problems other people tell you about. Kept in our hearts they either weigh us down or we shut off our emotions. Handed over to God, they're immediately in safe hands.

- Here's a tricky one – on the basis that Christ is to be found in each

person, try to receive the next person you meet as a gift from God. And the next one!

QUOTES

True spirituality is not a leisure-time activity, a diversion from life. It's essentially subversive and the test of its genuineness is practical.

Kenneth Leech

Heel that ball, Kelham, to the glory of God! Heel that ball to the glory of God!
Father Kelly, the Principal of Kelham Theological College, getting carried away at a rugby match

PRAYER

Lord God our Father
who with cross and nails won our full salvation
wield well your tools in this the workshop of your world,
that we who come to you rough hewn
may be fashioned into a greater likeness of your Son
Jesus Christ our Lord.

Markers on the way:
1 THE MODEL PRAYER

If we're asking about prayer, we might as well go to the top. Let's ask Jesus himself how to pray. It's what the disciples did (Luke 11.1–4) and they got this inspired answer – the Lord's own prayer. So if we're trying to take praying seriously we'll want to make use of this prayer, the best-known prayer in the world. It's prayed millions of times every day, and it leads us to the heart of the mystery of prayer, if only we'll pause long enough to notice. A naval officer was once praying the Lord's Prayer with a friend in a remote corner of Iceland. 'Say it slowly,' he said. 'Each phrase weighs a ton.' So let's look at each ton.

Our Father in heaven. Jesus could obviously call God 'Father'. The extraordinary thing is that he told us we could do the same! The word in Aramaic is a very intimate one – Abba, Dad. As we continue to claim that very close relationship with God, so we may become more like Jesus, the older brother, who fits that relationship perfectly. As we practise saying Abba, maybe practice will make perfect and we'll gradually become more Christlike.
Hallowed be your name. 'May your name be holy.' May your name be recognized as holy all over the place. May the world which recognizes 'holi-

ness' in all the wrong things – worshipping money, sex and power, for example – recognize true holiness. And let it start with me. May my vision be filled with the beauty and tenderness of God.
Your kingdom come, on earth as it is in heaven. This is the most exciting phrase in the whole Lord's Prayer. If God's kingdom is to come on earth we may need a few adjustments here first! It's not a phrase to trot out in church on Sunday without at least a crash helmet and a first-aid kit. This is serious praying for God's massive attack on all that frustrates his good and loving purposes. Are we ready to join in, and to have him start by working on us?
Give us this day our daily bread. In the kingdom or reign of God, each will have

what he or she needs. The future festival meal of the kingdom is something we can anticipate by asking specifically for whatever 'bread' we need, now, today. But we can't pray for that without bringing with us to the same table the hungry of the world whose need is simply that – bread. What, then, will we ourselves do about that need? (Is this prayer beginning to hurt?)

Forgive us our sins, as we forgive those who sin against us. One of our daughters used to come back from school repeating confidently: 'Forgive us our sings.' Presumably 'as we forgive those who sing against us!' But forgiveness is at the heart of Jesus' message. Not the easy tolerance of our age but the rich, hard, shocking, even reckless forgiveness which God gives us – if we but knew it. But we won't even recognize that forgiveness unless we too are living that way in relation to others. So how's it going?!

Lead us not into temptation. As if he would! But the temptation he speaks of isn't to do with some minor private sin, it's that we shouldn't be taken into the clutches of the greater darkness that opposes God's reign of love all over the world. This is more serious stuff. We need God to **deliver us from evil** as part of his great movement to deliver his precious and fragile world from its despair. Evil has to be confronted with the power of the cross, and that's where we have to take our stand as we grapple with our own temptations.

For the kingdom, the power and the glory are yours, now and for ever.

Thank goodness! The outcome of our struggle isn't in doubt. We can raise our eyes to the coming dawn because nothing can ultimately hold back the reign of God. Do we believe that?

TRY THIS

- When you pray the Lord's Prayer have a particular situation in mind as you go through each of the petitions. For instance, when praying 'hallowed be your name', think of the office or school where God's name is often only a swear word. When praying 'your kingdom come', think of the trouble spot where God's kingdom of peace is being so strongly resisted. When praying 'give us this day our daily bread', think of the pressing needs of some members of your family.
- You can take a different phrase each day and live with it as a special focus of prayer to be repeated or 'chewed' through the day. For example, what might 'your will be done' mean through the whole day if you tried to apply it to ordinary conversations, business transactions or time with friends?
- When praying the Lord's Prayer with others you can stop at a particular phrase and hold an extended silence while you all meditate upon it, before resuming the rest of the prayer.
- At the very least we can say the prayer more slowly and actually think about what we're saying!

STORY

Karl Marx's daughter once said to a friend that she hadn't been brought up with any religion and therefore wasn't religious. 'But the other day I came across a beautiful little prayer which I very much wish could be true,' she said. Asked what that prayer was, slowly she began repeating, 'Our Father, who art in heaven ...'

TEXT-MESSAGE LORD'S PRAYER

The Ship of Fools website had a competition to re-write the Lord's Prayer in mobile phone text message. One of the shortest entries went like this: God@heaven.org *You rule, up and down. We need grub and a break. Will pass it on. Keep us focused. You totally rule, long term. Amen.*

PART TWO: DAY BY DAY

6 HOW TO START THE DAY WITH GOD

Drive down any street in Britain today and you see a forest of little black satellite dishes turning their eager faces towards the skies. They represent a huge amount of enjoyment funnelling into those homes – and maybe a tiny bit of wasted time! In my imagination I'd like to think that all over the country at the start of the day there are even more minds and hearts turning towards God, like human satellite dishes, open to receive all the good things he has for us.

As soon as our feet hit the carpet in the morning we're on the go. Familiar routines slot into place. People flit in and out of bathrooms, bedrooms and kitchens by some unspoken, sophisticated choreography. A small variation in the expected moves ('Martin, will you please get up **now!**') causes a major breakdown in the system. Breakfast is a time of clipped conversation about marmalade, tetchy reminders about sports kit, and the dog always being in the wrong place, all to the background of an argument about politics on the radio. So where does prayer fit into this lot?

The key is regularity. It doesn't matter whether our way of starting the day with God is a snatched greeting or an extended conversation – the important thing is that it becomes part of the choreography of the morning. We don't have to think each morning about whether we're going to clean our teeth or not, because it's part of the routine. We just do it, without agonizing, and we know we're the better for it. So with prayer.

There's a short way and a long way to start the day with God. With a young family or an early start we'll probably simply want to place the day in God's hands and then get on with it. If the day is our own or we're retired we might want to make this the main time of prayer and spiritual input. But then again, temperament comes into it. Some of us like to settle into a longer, reflective time with God, while that drives others of us to chew the dog basket. Horses for courses; patterns for people.

So we may find it best to pray briefly by the washbasin while cleaning our teeth, or while walking the dog, or while commuting to work. Alternatively we might have fifteen minutes in the kitchen before anyone else comes down, or a relaxed time after breakfast when everything is quiet. The important principle is to make the time a regular one, and in it to place all the day – its events, its conversations, its work, its emotions – into God's safe hands. Then whatever happens in the day, we know he's there.

And all we've had to do is switch on the satellite receiver.

KEY QUESTION

Are you a morning person? If not, how will you switch on the satellite receiver?

TRY THIS (THE SHORT ROUTE)

• Just before you get out of bed or when you're in the bathroom or getting dressed, run through the day in your mind and ask God to guide and keep you through it. 'Lord, this is my day. These are my tasks, and these are my problems. Please just be there and get me through it well and graciously. Got to go – we'll have a longer chat later.'

• When you're walking – with the dog, or going to school or to work – use the time for a relaxed conversation with God. (You can even do this in the car – with care.) Be thankful for anything that strikes you as good, which might be a relationship, an absorbing interest, or the sun glinting on the dew. Run through some of the issues you and others around you are facing, and commend them to God, for his love to be at work in them. And offer the day ahead to God, for him to fill it with good things (or with survival!).

• You could establish a short three-stage routine, even when lying in bed just before you get up.
  1 Repeat the verse from Colossians 3.17: 'Whatever you do, in word or deed, do everything in the name of the Lord Jesus, giving thanks to God the Father through him.'
  2 Then think about the day ahead, asking God's help to do just that – to do everything in the name of Jesus.
  3 Then a standard prayer: 'Lord, I offer this day to you, the work I do, the people I meet, the pleasures and the problems, that in everything I may know the love of Christ, and be thankful. Amen.'

TRY THIS (THE LONG ROUTE)

If you are OK in the mornings, or at least prepared to admit that mornings exist, you might like to commit some proper time to your relationship with God before the day has tripped you up. Some people get up early and luxuriate in the calm of this quiet hour. Others use the time after breakfast if they don't have to go out. For ideas on what you might do with this time, see Section 8: 'How to use a special time of prayer'.

QUOTES

Prayer is the victory of mind over mattress.

John Perkins

The very moment you wake up each morning, all your wishes and hopes for the day rush at you like wild animals. And the first job each morning consists in shoving them all back; in listening to that other voice, taking that other point of view, letting that other larger, stronger, quieter life come flowing in. And so on, all day. We can only do it for moments at first. But from those moments the new sort of life will be spreading through our systems because now we are letting him work at the right part of us.

C. S. Lewis

In the morning, while it was still very dark he [Jesus] got up and went out to a deserted place, and there he prayed.

Mark 1.35

PRAYER

Lord, let your blessing be upon me as I begin
*   this day with you.*
Confirm me in the truth by which I rightly
*   live:*
Confront me with the truth from which I
*   wrongly turn.*
I ask not for what I want, but for what you
*   know I need,*
As I offer this day and myself for you and to
*   you*
In Jesus' name.

Iona (adapted)

7 HOW TO PRAY THROUGH THE DAY

So the day has begun, and we're off into a full-length feature film which could be called *Gone with the Wind*. Because that's how it goes for many of us – like the wind, and the thought of praying our way through it seems pretty unrealistic. But maybe we have our sights set too high. Prayer in the midst of the day may have to be done on the run, so it isn't a 'holy half-hour' we're looking for, but a series of momentary pit-stops. If we check our e-mail several times a day, couldn't we check in with God several times a day as well?

In this sense, prayer through the day is more like punctuation, the odd comma here, inverted commas there, a short period in brackets when the pace slows down for a bit, an occasional question mark where we find ourselves facing an important issue, one or two exclamation marks where wonder, surprise or humour breaks through, and finally a full stop when the day slows right down to its end. God has been fully present throughout the day, and our punctuation-prayer has simply kept us in touch. It's the 'chatting' prayer referred to in Section 5.

Behind this breathless attempt to get everything done, however, can be a deeper sense of prayerfulness. Not articulated in conscious prayer or even in God-thoughts, but in that deeper confidence that God is somehow always around and that everything is basically OK. It's that 'just getting on with it' prayer referred to in Section 5 again, getting on with life against the sure background of God's graceful presence. At the start of the day we put on our clothes and then more or less forget them. Similarly we can (as Paul says in Romans 13.14) 'put on the Lord Jesus Christ' and then get on with the day.

KEY QUESTION

What are your best ways of keeping in touch with God during a busy day?

TRY THIS

- Arrow prayers go straight to the heart. 'Lord, help!' is a well-known one, whether we're facing an interview, a difficult task, or a dentist's drill. 'Lord, help that person!' is another, when you see someone in the crowd struggling with a disability or with a tribe of recalcitrant children. As we walk down our own road we can pray for our neighbours as we pass each house, even if we don't know them. An ambulance streaking through the traffic is another call to pray. Arrow prayers are plentiful, fast and effective.
- Being thankful for a dozen or so good moments in a day is another way of locking on to God. The smell of freshly ground coffee or newly cut grass, the sight of early morning sunlight touching the trees, the uninhibited smile of a child, the sense of satisfaction when that job finally gets finished. Once we start noticing those gifts, we come to realize just how many there are, and it can all get rather intoxicating!
- A seventeenth-century French monk called Brother Lawrence became famous for his teaching on 'practising the presence of God', (see the quote below). He worked in the kitchens and claimed that he was as much at home with God there as in the chapel. He taught that we should practise our awareness of God's presence until it becomes habitual. In practical terms that means simply glancing in God's direction during the day, remembering his presence, being grateful, here and now, and doing everything 'for God'. What does that mean? Well, when we fall in love we tend to want to do everything 'for' the one we love. It's similar. It's not doing new things, but rather doing for God what we normally do for ourselves. Through all of this we can become so aware of the reality of God that his presence just becomes part of our mental and emotional furniture.
- We need to keep heaven and earth tied together, so referring the things of earth to the Lord of heaven is an important task, and the more 'earthy' those things are the more I think God might appreciate them! He probably

gets fairly bored with bland general-
izations in our prayers. When we hear
the news, or read the headlines, what
better than to pass on our concern
straight to God? When we talk to a
friend and hear of her struggle with
something, we can instantly put it into
God's in-tray. When we look at the
diary and wonder how to get through
it all, we can hand it over to God's
'eternal changelessness'. Real events
are the best basis for real prayers.

- I have a small wooden cross in my
coat pocket which is shaped to fit
comfortably into my hand. When I
plunge my hand in my coat pocket,
therefore, I'm instantly in touch with
the most powerful symbol this world
has known. For me, it's a reminder of
God's love and engagement with the
world that I'm walking through, so as
I walk, I can pray. Hand-crosses are
available from some religious
bookshops and retreat houses. Or you
could carve your own!

- We live in a world of background
music, so why shouldn't that music be
Christian? There's a huge range of
music CDs and tapes available for
every taste, whether it be classical,
modern chorus, Taizé, Iona, or even
modern 'crossover' music. Played in
the car, in the kitchen or anywhere
else, this music can be a reminder of
the life of the spirit in the heart of the
everyday.

- In the Eastern Orthodox Church there
is a famous prayer known as the Jesus
Prayer which people will repeat for
short or long periods. It goes like this:

'Lord Jesus Christ, Son of the living
God, have mercy on me, a sinner.' It
can keep us focused on Jesus Christ
whatever we're doing and reminds us
of our dependence on him at all times.
A rosary works in the same way.

QUOTES

The time of action does not differ from
that of prayer. I possess God as
peacefully in the bustle of my kitchen,
where sometimes several people are
asking me for different things at the
same time, as I do upon my knees
before the blessed sacrament. This
practice of the presence of God must
stem from the heart, from love. Love
does everything, and it is not necessary
to have great things to do. I turn my
little omelette in the pan for the love of
God. When it is finished, if I have
nothing to do, I prostrate myself on the
ground and worship my God, who
gave me this grace to make it, after
which I arise happier than a king.
When I can do nothing else, it is
enough to have picked up a straw for
the love of God. People look for ways
of learning how to love God. They
hope to attain it by I know not how
many different practices. They take
much trouble to abide in his presence
by varied means. Is it not a shorter and
more direct way *to do everything for
the love of God*, to make use of all the
tasks one's lot in life demands to show
him that love, and to maintain his
presence within by the communion of

our hearts with his? There is nothing complicated about it. One only has to turn to it honestly and simply.

Brother Lawrence

Rejoice always, pray without ceasing, give thanks in all circumstances, for this is the will of God in Christ for you.

1 Thessalonians 5.16–18

PRAYER

O Lord, you know how busy I must be this day;
If I forget you, do not you forget me, for Christ's sake.

Lord Astley (before the Battle of Edgehill)

You should have gone before you got up there!

8 HOW TO USE A SPECIAL TIME OF PRAYER

We've looked at 'just getting on with it' prayer and 'chatting' prayer in the last section. What we come to look at now is 'talking' prayer, what to do in the time we've set aside especially to focus on our relationship with God. Without some such dedicated time that relationship is likely to suffer as much as a human relationship that isn't valued properly or given enough time and attention. It may not be possible to find that time every day, but it has to be found on some days or we'll notice the difference. The concert pianist Artur Rubinstein once said: 'If I don't practise for a day, I notice the difference; if I don't practise for two days, my family notices the difference; if I don't practise for three days, the public notices the difference.'

When? The most important thing here is regularity. It doesn't matter when the time is, as long as it's regular. Depending on our life-situation, it could be early in the morning (there are such people, I'm told), in the commuter train, after getting the children off to school, during a lunch break in a park or a city church, after supper if we're not going out, or maybe last thing at night. For a student it could be when you first get to your desk. For other people it could be when walking the dog, or cooking, or even changing the baby's nappy. (Be gentle with yourself if you have a young family – it's the most difficult time of all to sustain a life of prayer.) We have to be flexible in our timing but this period of prayer needs to become a regular part of our life rather than an extra we might easily forget.

Where? What we need here is somewhere that becomes associated with prayer, so that simply to go to that place takes us halfway into the presence of God already. The particular place may be a chair by the window or in the kitchen; it may be a corner of a room, set up to be a special 'chapel'; it may even be a seat on the train or in the car, or a particular part of a walk. Places are more significant than many people think. We all of us have special places – be they football grounds, the setting of a first romance, the scene of a glorious holiday. And sacred places, too, matter very much – places where heaven has opened a crack, where an angel's wing has brushed our face, or where we've experienced mystery. There are no rules about where our special place should be, at home, in a church or in a field. But when you get there – stay. The philosopher Pascal said: 'Most of the troubles of man come from him not being able to stay alone in his own room.' In other words, there is serious business to be done here – don't run away.

With what things? If we are going to have our own space at home then a number of questions arise about what we'll need with us. Again, this is very much up to personal choice. Many of us value having a cross at the centre of our vision, or an icon. Candles speak a common language and lighting a candle marks out the time we're giving to this special purpose of prayer. Something of beauty may help – flowers are common. We may also have a small CD or cassette player to play appropriate music as we settle in. A simple prayer stool where you tuck your legs under the cross-piece is comfortable and relaxed. And of course we need the Bible with us, and maybe a few other devotional books to help our prayer and reflection. This is a place to be at home in, so the choices we make are very personal. In the centre of my own sacred space, under the cross, is a pair of pottery hands I got on the Greek island of Patmos. These open hands are a constant symbol of my need to open myself to God, and also to place in his hands the needs and issues of the day.

KEY QUESTION

How organized do you want to be in your special-time praying?

TRY THIS

I'm offering here three ways of using this special time of prayer: a Quiet Time, a Service of Daily Prayer, and Open Space.

- *A Quiet Time.* This usually means spending time with the Bible and some Bible-reading notes, and letting this lead into prayer. There are many sources of Bible-reading notes, and some are listed in the Resources section at the end of the book. Classically the way to use the time is
  1 pray for insight and wisdom;
  2 read the Bible passage for the day;
  3 ponder what you've read to see what it says to you;
  4 read the notes and ponder again;
  5 pray out of all you've thought and read.

  The Quiet Time has a long and honourable tradition. Its great strength is that it gets us into reading the scriptures and applying their timeless wisdom and truth to our own day and our own lives. Prayer inevitably flows out of that encounter with the Bible.

- *A Service of Daily Prayer.* This service, traditionally called an 'office', is a short, structured service of psalms, Bible readings and prayers which has been part of the life of the Church for centuries. The prayer carries you along no matter how you're feeling, and puts you before God in words and forms which you haven't had to create. The danger may be that we get into unthinking repetition, but the advantage is that we are held steadily before God and fed, almost unconsciously, with the things of God. Examples of services of daily prayer are the Anglican *Common Worship* service which succeeds the Alternative Service Book, the Franciscan

Celebrating Common Prayer, and the Celtic Daily Office from the Northumbria Community (see Resources section).

- *Open Space.* Here are some other ways we can use that special time.

1 *Centring, receiving, praying*

To centre ourselves we need to take four steps. First, to make ourselves comfortable but alert; second, to relax the body, and particularly the places of tension in us; third, to listen to the sounds around us, further away and close by; and fourth, to open ourselves to God.

To receive we could read the Bible or any spiritual book we choose. The Bible is central, but I also sometimes read a book of sermons, poetry, devotional classics or books of meditations (see Resources).

To pray we could use any of the ways of praying in this book or elsewhere. Eventually words may give out and silence take over. That's fine. And don't go until you've finished!

2 *Music and silence*

You may respond very much to a certain type of music and simply want to play it quietly as an aid to worship and reflection. Then let the silence take over, and in the open space talk, listen or just look. You might use a picture or icon rather than music. Rembrandt's *Return of the Prodigal Son* proved a rich source of inspiration to Henri Nouwen in his book of that name and to thousands of others because of it.

An image

What are we doing when we pray in all these different ways? A friend gave me this image based on the parable of the man who built his house on the rock (Matthew 7.24–7). When we pray it's as if we are putting down spiritual boreholes. At first they go down into sand, which is often what our prayer feels like to begin with – nothing solid, a waste of time, lost in our own meanderings. But as we keep going down we eventually hit rock, which is where Jesus told us to build our foundations, on God himself. However, as we keep putting the borehole deeper and deeper, we may well come to the level of molten rock which shoots up the borehole and catches us by surprise. So it is with the Spirit: God is not only solid as rock, he's also powerful, energetic and life-giving, and he may surprise us with the force of his presence.

Our task in prayer, then, is to keep putting the borehole down, through our human weaknesses (the sand) and into the reality of God (the rock), eventually perhaps getting through to the surprises of the Spirit (the molten rock) where God comes shooting to the surface and we are caught up for a moment in the joy and wonder of his divine life.

PRAYER

Almighty God, you have made us for yourself, and our hearts are restless till they find rest in you. Grant us purity of heart and strength of purpose, that no selfish passion may hinder us from knowing your will, and no weakness hinder us from doing it; but that in your light we may see light, and in your service find our perfect freedom; through Jesus Christ our Lord.

St Augustine

He says he's having his quiet time...

9 HOW TO PRAY FOR OTHER PEOPLE

I wonder how many requests God receives in an average day? It will certainly run into hundreds of millions. Cyberspace is constantly packed with prayer, delivered to that well-known address www.Jesus.com. Christians call this praying for others 'intercession', and it's the most common form of prayer. Indeed, it's what many people think you mean when you talk about prayer – forgetting all the other prayer such as giving thanks, being sorry, and silently resting in God.

But that's fine with God. He takes whatever we offer and works with it, and if we come with a list of requests, he might well say: 'Fair enough. It's what Jesus told them to do. Ask and you'll receive, seek and you'll find, knock and the door will fly open' (Luke 11.9).

Sometimes, of course, we do rather take advantage of that promise. An eighteenth-century businessman prayed like this: 'O Lord, who knowest I have mine estates in the City of London, and likewise that I have lately purchased an estate in the county of Essex, I beseech thee to preserve the two counties of Middlesex and Essex from fire and earthquake. For the rest of the counties thou mayest deal with them as thou art pleased.'

Fortunately God isn't proud and he takes all our prayers and uses them, sometimes having to work quite hard to pull them round to make some sort of sense! He may have to answer the deeper prayer rather than the superficial one we actually put to him. He may have to resist the role of magician. But he still honours and uses our deep instinct to pray.

When we pray for others what makes it so special is that it's a way of loving them. It's the best and biggest thing we can do for anyone, to hold them before God and expose them to the power of love, the power which, after all, makes and sustains the world. So saying that we'll pray for someone is a serious commitment to loving that person enough to take them regularly to God. It isn't a spiritual sticking plaster to enable us to make a clean getaway.

The basis of our prayer for other people is that fundamentally we all belong to one another, so 'if one part of the body suffers, all suffer together with it' (1 Corinthians 12.26). If you think of the earth's crust without any oceans, all parts of the world are joined. As John Donne wrote: 'No man is an island, entire of itself; every man is a piece of the continent, a part of the main.' So we are joined, we belong, and that makes intercession both natural for us to offer, and possible for God to use.

But I'd like to raise the stakes a bit and suggest that prayer for the world, and for others in it, is no less than joining in God's majestic project to transform the world. It isn't about finding lost car keys or curing Aunt Mabel's ingrowing toenail. It's making ourselves part of God's massive attack on evil and on everything that destroys, distorts or cramps human life. Wherever Jesus found evil in his ministry he opposed it, and he invited his disciples (and all Rabbit's friends and relations) to join in the campaign. It was a campaign of love, and by our prayer we can be part of that campaign now.

KEY QUESTION

Do we care enough for people and situations, whether near at hand or in the news, to pray for them?

JOKE BOX

One evening young Ben asked his father for a pet. 'Sorry,' said his father, 'not now. But if you pray really hard for two months, perhaps God will send you a baby brother.' So Ben prayed for a month, but it seemed futile so he gave up.

However, a month later a new baby arrived – or so Ben thought. His father drew back the covers and showed Ben – twins. 'Aren't you glad you prayed for a baby brother?' asked his father. 'I certainly am,' said Ben, 'and aren't you glad I stopped praying when I did!'

TRY THIS

- The time-honoured way to pray for others is to make a list so we don't forget anyone. A small notebook might help, with space for different sections (regulars, special situations, world news, church). Whether the list is kept long or short is a matter of our choice. I prefer a short list and I only pray for so many people on it at any one time, leaving the rest of the names at the foot of the cross or in the pottery hands (see above, Section 8). Lists need to be renewed or they become unmanageable. We could burn the list prayerfully at the start of Lent, Advent and other times, commending the names carefully to God's keeping as we do so.
- We might use sticky notelets in a special place such as a noticeboard in the kitchen, or a cupboard door, having a different name on each one. Individual names can then be brought into prominence, or removed, or grouped, or changed. Confidentiality needs to be respected when names are in a semi-public place.
- Try a 'handful of prayer'. The five (or ten) fingers and thumbs can each represent a special person you want to pray for. Anywhere, anytime, you can then call to mind those five people and pray for them, placing them 'in the palm of God's hand' (Isaiah 49.16).
- Names and concerns can be written on separate small pieces of card and these all kept in a bowl. We can then take out a few cards each day, even perhaps carrying them with us through the day and returning them to the bowl at the end of the day. Seeing the name or feeling the piece of card in the pocket then reminds us to pray for them during the day.
- We could have photos of some of the special people we're committed to pray for, and keep them in our prayer place. The photos can then be taken out one at a time and our prayers for those people can seem considerably more vivid because another of our senses is engaged.
- My father used to use his Christmas cards as his reminders for prayer. Each day five or six cards would be taken off the pile and the people prayed for. These people, after all, were the ones he had a closer relationship with and would want to support in prayer.
- For those with a well-developed imagination other methods can come into play. We can, for example, bring people in our mind's eye to meet Jesus, and then step back and watch. Jesus may gently lay his hands on that person in a touch, an embrace or a

blessing. They may talk, or weep or laugh. We mustn't force it. When Jesus lets the person go, we might then bring another.

- When you have a particular person to pray for in a time of special need, you could prayerfully light a candle in your room and let the fragrance of the prayer continue for as long as it's needed, or as long as it's safe for the candle to burn.

STORY

In 1938 a monk died on Mount Athos. He was a very simple man who'd been in charge of some of the workshops in the monastery, which were manned by young Russians who came for a year or two to make some money to take back to their villages so that they could marry or build a hut or plant some crops. One day some of the other monks who were in charge of other workshops said, 'Father Silouan, how is it that the men who work with you work so well even though you never supervise them, while we spend our time looking after our workmen and they're always trying to cheat us?'

'I don't know,' said Father Silouan. 'I can only tell you what I do. When I come in the morning I never come without having prayed for these people and I come with my heart filled with love and compassion for them, and when I walk into the workshop I have tears in my soul for them. And then I give them the day's task, and I say as

There was a brief discussion on whether to pray or run.

long as they'll work I'll pray for them. So I go to my cell and I pray for them individually. I say, "Lord, remember Nicholas. He's only 20 and he's left his young wife and child in the village. Can you imagine the misery there, that made him come here? Protect them in his absence. Shield them from evil. Give him courage for this year so he can go back to a wonderful reunion."'

And he said, 'In the beginning I pray with tears of compassion but then the sense of the divine presence grows on me and eventually it grows so powerful that I lose sight of Nicholas and his wife and child and his village, and I'm only aware of God, and I'm drawn deeper and deeper into the divine presence, until at the heart of the presence I meet the divine love holding Nicholas and his wife and child. And now it's with the love of God that I begin to pray for them again. And so,' he said, 'I spend my days praying for each of them in turn, and when the day is over I go and have a few words with them, we pray together and they go to their rest. And I go back to my monastic office.'

Anthony Bloom, School for Prayer

10 HOW TO END THE DAY WITH GOD

So we've got to the end of the day! The pace slackens; darkness falls. It's like a car slowing down as it comes off the motorway, or a ship nosing its way into port. We're 'coming home' at the end of the day.

For many people this is a good time to pray because there's plenty of 'stuff' to pray about. In particular this is a good time to review the day, to see it in the light of God, and so perhaps to grow in personal and spiritual awareness. By looking back on the day, thoughtfully and prayerfully, we might become more aware of God's footprints through the day, and we might even come to know ourselves a little better.

The crucial activity is *reflection*, which is simply looking at the past and trying to learn from it. Ronald Knox, a translator of the Bible, was a very precocious child, and he often couldn't get to sleep at night. When he was four years old his parents asked him what he did when he couldn't sleep and he answered, with all the seriousness and experience of his four years, 'I lie there and I think about the past.' At least he had the right idea! Someone said, 'The unreflected life is not worth living.' That may be a bit extreme, but the point is well made that thinking through what we have experienced is a huge resource for living in the future.

There are certain classic ways of thinking about the day and about how our life is going, for example, the method of St Ignatius (see below). But there are others. The important thing is to note the 'hot spots' in the day when something special was going on, and to examine them for whatever truth and insight they have to offer.

And apart from that, night time is often just a good time to be with God, to give thanks, to pray for others, and to say goodnight!

KEY QUESTION

Where were today's hot spots? Where were your emotions most strongly engaged (for good or ill) and where, in retrospect, was God's presence most clear?

TRY THIS

- Run through the day like a video, remembering the sequence of events – the people you met, the tasks you did, the conversations you had, places you went, TV programmes you watched, etc. As you go through, freeze frame the action at good moments to give thanks, at moments when you messed up to say sorry, at moments when you met people with problems to pray for them, and so on. You don't have to laboriously cover every incident! Nevertheless we're rounding off the day, bringing it back into relation to God and into his keeping.

- Do a more general sweep over the day looking for the one or two key events – a bit like sweeping a metal detector over an area of ground, listening for the places where the machine gets excited. When you identify the hot spots you can turn them over in your mind in the presence of God and try to discover what was really going on there, why you reacted as you did, what were the deeper emotions stirred in you, and what you might do in the future in response to all that. The key question, and one not to evade, is: 'What is God saying through all this?'

- Try what's called the *Examen* of St Ignatius. It's a structured way of reflecting on the day and trying to discern where God has been moving in it and in you.

  1 First be still and remember God. He is present, right now.

  2 Ask God to shine his light over the day and into your heart so you can see clearly what's been going on.

  3 Think through the day, but more than the events, be aware of your feelings. Were you joyful, sad, fearful, angry, bewildered? Why might that be? God guides us through our moods and feelings. Normally his way is peaceful and consoling, so if you were

disturbed, can you tell where that unease was coming from? Feelings are surface emotions; moods lie just under the surface, like tides under the waves. Where are the tides coming from, and why?

Think positively about what you did well today (there will always be something!) and give thanks. But also, think if you turned away from the way of God at particular points, and ask for forgiveness and new strength.

Look forward to tomorrow with hope, because God will be with you all through the day and it will be full of possibilities.

Writing a journal

Some people find it very helpful to keep a journal of their inner life and thoughts to help them express their feelings and perhaps give some shape to their experiences. Some people write a little every day, others at particular periods of change, or when they're on a retreat. We can write absolutely whatever we want. Perhaps we want to capture an experience of God or of the opposite, spiritual desolation. Perhaps we want to articulate something going on in us and in our thinking. Perhaps we want to remember something that was said or something that happened, or we want to record what we're praying about or feeling strongly about. The exercise of writing can be helpful in itself, and it's

fascinating reading it later and seeing what was going on in us at particular times – and seeing what God has done with us since! All we need is a special notebook and the determination to start.

Puzzled by prayer?

So we've reached the end of the day and the last five sections of this book have been suggesting all sorts of ways of praying 'day by day'. But maybe you're feeling this is all a bit too much like hard work, or a bit too much like travelling in alien territory. You only wanted to think a bit more about spirituality, and you've ended up with loads of methods and techniques of praying. If so, let me suggest two reassurances at this point:

1 Prayer actually has no rules. It's simply the meeting of a human being with his or her Maker. Pray as you can, not as you can't. Be yourself, because God can't deal with you if you're not.
2 There's a great promise in Paul's letter to the Christians in Rome which says that when we pray it's actually the Spirit praying in us anyway. He knows what he's doing, so why not relax and get on with it, trusting him to sort out the details? The actual promise goes like this:

The Spirit helps us in our weakness, for we do not know how to pray as we ought, but that very Spirit intercedes with sighs too deep for words. And God, who searches the heart, knows what is the mind of the Spirit, because the Spirit intercedes for the saints according to the will of God.

Romans 8.26–7

Prayer may be a puzzle but it's a profoundly simple puzzle and like anything else worth doing, from skiing to computing to training a puppy, it responds to regular practice!

PRAYER

Thanks be to thee, Lord Jesus Christ
for all the benefits which thou hast won for
* us,*
for all the pains and insults which thou hast
* borne for us.*
O most merciful Redeemer, Friend and
* Brother*
may we know thee more clearly,
love thee more dearly,
and follow thee more nearly,
day by day.

Richard of Chichester

Markers on the way:
2 PRAYER AND ACTION

A Bible full of holes

A theological student once took an old Bible and a pair of scissors and cut out of the Bible every reference to the poor, or God's concern for the marginalized, or God's demand for justice for the oppressed. It took him a very long time but when he'd finished, the Bible literally fell apart. It was a Bible full of holes.

Some people who have read this far may be getting impatient. It may seem to them that prayer is an activity too cut off from the risks and struggles of ordinary life. It may even seem as if prayer is an escape into a pink mist of personal spirituality, where the consolations of the inner life substitute for the harder realities of twenty-first-century living.

Contrast this with the words of theologian Kenneth Leech. 'True spirituality is not a leisure-time activity, a diversion from life. It is essentially subversive, and the test of its genuineness is practical.' Or the famous theologian Karl Barth: 'To clasp the hands in prayer is the beginning of an uprising against the disorder of the world.' There must be a direct link between how we pray and how we act. It isn't sufficient to pray away happily in our own quiet spaces without engaging with the needs and the pain of society.

The reason for this is clear. Contact with the living God is bound to propel us into action, just as the relationship of Jesus with his heavenly Father propelled him into healing the unhealed, touching the untouchable, and meeting the marginalized on their own ground. His message wasn't about self-fulfilment, self-actualization or any other self-centred therapy; it was about a kingdom of justice, mercy and peace. He declared that this kingdom of God was breaking in, there and then, and he challenged people to join up to that great project. He didn't come with a spiritual duvet but with a spiritual alarm-clock.

What does this mean for prayer?

- You could pray about world issues, straight from the news. Use your imagination to envisage the human cost. Struggle with God and with yourself if you find points of resistance and confusion as you pray. As Jacob struggled with the divine stranger through the night, don't let go!
- Listen to the niggling voice in your heart that tells you to get on and do something about some of these things you see and hear of. Let the environmental crisis get you involved with Friends of the Earth; let the rough sleepers in your city get you involved with a night shelter; let a friend in despair lead you to go on a listening course.
- See prayer as a dangerous activity. Peace worker Daniel Berrigan: 'The time will shortly be upon us, if it is not already here, when the pursuit of contemplation becomes a strictly subversive activity.' Martin Luther King talked about Christians needing to be 'creatively maladjusted' to the prevailing norms of society. The reason is that true prayer purifies the mind and heart of the layers of self-deception which become caked over the soul. Prayer should strip down our spiritual lives to basics, and there we might discover the resources to resist injustice.
- Determine that when you pray for someone in need that you will also ask the question, 'And is there something I could do to be part of answering my own prayer?' It may be sending a card assuring them of your love and prayer; it may be making a meal for a stressed family; it may be going and taking their ironing away, or just going and listening. There may not be much you can actually do in some situations, but ask the question anyway.
- When you read the life of Jesus in the Gospels, read it in the light of the central gospel proclamation, 'The kingdom of God is at hand.' If you can recognize the social and political challenge inherent in those words it will enliven your reading of the Gospels and your appreciation of the threat Jesus posed. This Jesus was dangerous, and his followers today should have something of that same whiff of danger about them! See Charles Elliott's classic *Praying the Kingdom*.

And what of the Church?

The future of the Church lies in being a community of protest rather than a society of religious self-preservation.
                                    Robert Jeffery

It is because the world is holy and good, but also twisted and disfigured, that certain places are set apart as redeemed areas, liberated zones, reclaimed from the forces of evil. The Church is a redeemed part of creation, not as a refuge

from the unredeemed world, but rather
as a foretaste of its redemption to come.
Kenneth Leech

An image

Charles de Foucauld founded the Little Brothers of Jesus in North Africa. He lived in what he called 'the frigate', a dwelling shaped like a juggernaut lorry. At one end of it was the altar, a rough wooden box with an open Bible resting on it. The other end of the building was permanently open so that anyone could come and go. He said that he met God at either end – at one end at the altar, and at the other end in his neighbour. And it reminded him that the purpose of prayer was to serve the world. (Eventually de Foucauld was killed by some of the local people he had come to serve.)

PRAYER

O God,
it is your will to hold both heaven and earth
in a single peace.
Let the design of your great love
shine on the waste of our wraths and
*   sorrows,*
and give peace to your Church,
peace among nations,
peace in our homes,
and peace in our hearts.
New Zealand Prayer Book

A BLESSING

And now to him who is able to keep us
from falling and lift us from the dark valley
of despair to the bright mountain of hope,
from the midnight of desperation to the
daybreak of joy; to him be power and
authority, for ever and ever.
Martin Luther King

PART THREE: GOOD PRACTICE

11 HOW TO PRAY WITH THE BIBLE

When the Christian faith first became real to me, one of my most important discoveries was the liveliness and relevance of the Bible. I really enjoyed reading it (the understandable parts!) and finding beautiful passages and exciting promises. I was only catching up with what every other Christian has always known! When the great Reformer Martin Luther said, 'The Bible is alive, it speaks to me; it has feet, it runs after me; it has hands, it lays hold on me,' he was reflecting the truth the Church has always known but which it often forgets, the truth that 'the word of God is living and active and sharper than any two-edged sword' (Hebrews 4.12).

This is our basic Christian handbook. It's not a book of rules – though it has some. It's not a book of religious techniques – though it has lots of practical ideas. It's not a codebook for the initiated – though it has plenty of puzzles for theologians. It's essentially a book about a relationship – a relationship between God and his wayward people – and what God has done to restore and develop that relationship. As such, it's bound to be of huge value in prayer, because prayer is a relationship too, between us and God, an arena of love and loyalty, struggle and failure, discovery and delight.

The Bible is a kind of companion to prayer, a friend who we love and trust, even if we don't always understand or even agree. But all the time we're learning about ourselves and about the divine Author, the playwright who's partly writing the play as we go along and who's also the director who inspires the best performances from his cast.

We come to the Bible not just to study but to pray.

KEY QUESTION

Have you ever used the Bible regularly in prayer? Have you tried anchoring your prayer in these sacred words? And if so, are you prepared to take a few more risks in how you use it?

TRY THIS

- In Section 8 ('How to use a special time of prayer') there were some simple ways of reading the Bible and praying – the Quiet Time, a Service of Daily Prayer (a daily 'office') and Open Space. Now may be the time to re-visit those suggestions.
- Take a verse which has spoken to you from your reading of the Bible that morning or the night before, and carry

it with you as a kind of 'motto' for the day. You can repeat it from time to time by taking it out of your mental pocket and trying it for size. It will act as a reminder of the presence of God and – depending on the type of verse – it may encourage, inspire or challenge you.

For example, if you're reading Colossians 3, you could choose:

'Clothe yourselves with compassion, kindness, humility, meekness and patience.'

'Bear with one another and, if anyone has a complaint about another, forgive each other, just as the Lord has forgiven you.'

'Let the peace of Christ rule in your heart.'

'If you have been raised with Christ, seek the things that are above, where Christ is, seated at the right hand of God.' (Not recommended for long-distance lorry drivers!)

• One of the most tried and tested methods of praying with the Bible rejoices in the name *'lectio divina'*, or holy reading. It's as old as the fourth century, having been developed in the earliest communities of monks in the deserts of North Africa, and later finding classic expression in the communities of St Benedict. In its contemporary form it can best be described under three key words:

1 *Read.* Take a passage. You may be working your way through a letter of St Paul, or taking some of the psalms, or revisiting the Sermon on the Mount in Matthew 5—7. You begin reading slowly and attentively, until a phrase, or a word, or a whole verse arrests you. It won't take long! A phrase will soon pop up and ask to be taken more seriously.

2 *Reflect.* Now is the time of meditation, or chewing on this particular morsel. Repeat it, roll it around the mind, look at it from this way and that, repeat it again, gently suck all the goodness out of it. It's the process of reflection, trying to let the meaning of the phrase sink slowly from your head to your heart. Don't force it; just let the significance of those words emerge naturally within you. Taste the goodness.

3 *Respond.* When the reflection comes to a natural end, move into praying about the thoughts and understandings which have welled up inside you. This may mean you want to give thanks, or say sorry, or make a resolution before God, or hammer something out with him, or simply carry a burden silently to him. Stay with this time, too, until you've finished.

And then you may go back to the passage and move on, seeing which phrase pops its head up next. You can go on doing this, depending on how much time you have, but my experience is that it's quite an intense way of praying and you may not be able to repeat the process too many times. It can take quite a long time to get through the Bible this way – at least a lifetime! But if you decide not to repeat the process then you could move into a fourth and final phase:

4 *Rest.* This is the stage of stillness that flows out of prayer, as the words run out and silence and rest take over. There is more about this kind of still, silent prayer in Sections 17 ('How to soak in silence') and 18 ('How to enter the mystery').

QUOTE

Meditation on Scripture creates specially favourable conditions for God to speak to us and evoke our response, [which may be] of loving attention, gratitude, pain, desire, caring, offering, questioning, repenting, trusting, letting go, promising.

Martin L. Smith

STORY

A village woman in Tanzania always walked around with a bulky Bible. She would never be parted from it. The villagers often teased her. 'Why always the Bible?' they said. 'There are so many other books you could read!' But the woman simply smiled and carried on with her Bible. Finally, one day when they were teasing her again, she knelt down in the midst of them all and, holding the Bible above her head, she said with a big smile, 'Yes, of course there are many books which I could read. But there's only one book which reads me!'

So that's the book we can trust to lead us into prayer.

Jesus on prayer

Some of the classic teaching of Jesus on prayer is found in Luke 11.1–13. Here is wisdom in the shape of the Lord's Prayer, teaching about perseverance in prayer, and teaching about expectation. Similarly Matthew's main section on prayer is found in Matthew 6.5–15 which includes the Lord's Prayer but also Jesus' teaching about the style of our prayer and the importance of forgiveness.

We see how Jesus prayed in glimpses throughout the Gospels – how he went out by himself to the hills to pray (Matthew 14.23), often early in the morning (Mark 1.35); how he viewed prayer as the only way to deal with particular problems (Mark 9.29), and how he would pray with extreme intensity (Luke 22.40–4). John's Gospel gives us a sustained example of the prayer of Jesus in chapter 17.

It's clear that Jesus' whole life was based on his intimate relationship with his Father and that involved constant prayer. Prayerful dependence on God was the cornerstone of his life.

PRAYER

Blessed Lord,
who caused all holy scriptures to be written
*   for our learning:*
help us so to hear them,

to read, mark, learn and inwardly digest
   them
that, through patience, and the comfort of
   your holy word,
we may embrace and for ever hold fast

the hope of everlasting life,
which you have given us in our Saviour Jesus
   Christ.

Collect for the last Sunday
after Trinity

12 HOW TO PRAY WITH THE GOSPELS – THE IGNATIAN WAY

One of the most profound ways of encountering Jesus is through a form of prayer known as 'Ignatian meditation' after St Ignatius Loyola, who founded the Jesuits (Society of Jesus). In recent years this way of entering the events recorded in the Bible has proved popular with all sorts of people because it's an immediate, experiential and powerful way of praying – not just a Bible study involving the mind, but a living encounter with Christ involving the whole personality.

The essence of this way of praying is that we go into a Gospel event with all our senses of sight, smell, touch, hearing and taste. We go through the event as a participant, experiencing the smell of the sea air at Capernaum, the blazing sun on our head, the rough working clothes people have on, the look on people's faces. And so we watch the event from inside the story, not from reading pages in a book, and this in turn may bring us face to face with Jesus himself, and our conversation with him can be a most precious encounter and the most personal of prayers.

Not everyone finds they can get into this way of praying. It might feel a bit too fanciful at first, or a bit contrived. And indeed, it may be that this is not a way of prayer that will help you particularly. But it's worth persisting with this method for a while. When we overcome the strangeness and relax with it, this can be a profound and moving way of praying and it can lead to all kinds of discoveries about ourselves and about God.

KEY QUESTION

Are you alive?! Because if you are, your many different senses are automatically at work helping you to understand what's going on around you. They enable you to pick up the many layers and textures of a situation. This is all you need for Ignatian meditation – and perhaps a little more time than usual.

TRY THIS

Settle into a comfortable position – whatever is right for you (see Section 8). Choose a biblical story and read it through slowly and attentively. Then put the Bible down, close your eyes and re-run the story in your mind, but this time use all your senses and emotional responses to get inside the event – see the people, listen to what's being said and in what tone of voice, watch people respond, observe their body-language, notice how you're feeling, and so on.

Towards the end of the story it may be possible to move closer to Jesus (if the story is one with him in it, of course), and to get into a conversation with him about what has just happened, and what effect that had on you. Let that conversation (prayer) run as long as it will, before leaving Jesus again and carefully coming out of the situation. Reflect on what you have learnt and understood, and give God thanks.

An example: Jesus heals a paralysed man (Mark 2.1–12)

You're sitting in that house ... it's packed ... Look around at the crowd as people still try to squeeze in ... be aware of their clothes ... the rough cloth of the person next to you ... the look on

their faces ... The room is hot, dark with people ... but all facing in one direction... Follow their gaze ... look at the man they're all looking at ... What do you notice about him? ... look carefully ... What effect does he have on you?

Now listen to what that man is saying ... how is he speaking? Loud or soft, relaxed or urgent? Does he smile, laugh, frown? ... Look around at all the people again ... How are they responding? ...

A noise ... from up above? What's going on? ... What do you see as you look up? ... and what's the mood in the room as they see what's happening? ... Watch the delicate manoeuvring of the paralysed man as he comes down ... what do the people sitting underneath do? ... and look back at the teacher, Jesus ... How is he looking on at all of this? ... Is he amused, thoughtful, welcoming – or what?

The paralysed man is on the floor now ... Look at him carefully, at his expression, his disability ... What do you notice? ... And the men who have lowered him down ... where are they now? Doing what? ... Jesus is speaking to the man in a serious way ... what is he saying? ... Does what he says strike you as strange at all, or entirely natural?

Be aware now of a disturbance from a group of men in the corner ... Who are they? ... had you noticed them before? ... They seem to be objecting. Why? ... watch their body-language ... and watch the look on Jesus' face as well ... He's speaking to them again, firmly ... listen to the sharp exchange ... be aware of the atmosphere in the room ... Now Jesus speaks to the man on the camp-bed. Listen to the tone of voice ... watch the action unfold ... watch as the man picks up his camp-bed and makes his uncertain way out ...

A hubbub breaks out all over the room ... people are deep in excited conversation, amazed at what they've seen ... You're drawn towards Jesus, picking your way carefully over all the people ... Jesus seems to have been waiting for you ... he looks at you ... What do you see in his face? ... how do you feel? ... what do you want to say to him? ... Is it something about forgiveness? or healing? or what? ... What does he say to you in return? ... and in what way? ... and how do you respond to what he says? ... Don't rush this conversation ... time stands still ... just talk quietly together for as long as it takes ...

The time has come to step back ... time starts moving again ... work your way out of the crowded room ... into the cool of the night air ... Just stand there, or walk gently away, but whichever you do ... remember what you have just seen and heard ... remember and think ... that was important ... What will you do about it?

Just be quiet for a while now and rest in the presence of God.

St Ignatius Loyola

Inigo Loyola was a Spanish nobleman brought up in high society to be a soldier.

However, in 1521, when about 30, he had a sudden career change when he was recovering from a leg wound suffered in the siege of Pamplona. He read about the life of Christ and the lives of the saints and from then on wanted to give his life in service to Christ and to others. He wanted first to go to Jerusalem and in the two years he took getting there he wrote down different ways of prayer and meditation which helped him. This was the basis of the world-famous *Spiritual Exercises*, which made full use of the method of imaginative meditation outlined above.

Ignatius stayed in Jerusalem for only two weeks but he realized he needed to study a lot more, so he set about eight years of intensive study. In some of those years he was in trouble with the Inquisition but in 1534 he and a group of friends made a life vow of poverty and service, offering themselves to the Pope for whatever use he wanted. After ordination in Venice the group of ten friends made their way to Rome, and in 1540 they were constituted as the Society of Jesus by the Pope. The distinctive feature of this order was that they were not to be confined to monasteries but would go anywhere, do anything asked of them, and pray wherever they happened to be. They would 'find God in all things', said Ignatius in his *Constitutions* – in people, places and events.

The Jesuits grew rapidly, spreading through Europe, the Far East and Latin America, concentrating on preaching, spiritual direction, education and practical care. Ignatius died in 1556, but the

Jesuits were by then well established, and his method of praying through imaginative meditation on Bible pas- sages was to be just one of his lasting gifts to the Church and to the spiritual life.

13 HOW TO PRAY WITH THE COMMUNITY – THE BENEDICTINE WAY

Prayer often feels like a solitary experi- ence, something we do by ourselves, out of sight, personal and private. The truth is, however, that we never pray alone. Countless millions of people are praying at any given moment and our prayer is just one drop in the vast river of prayer which is always flowing towards God. Even if we are praying quietly in our own room, we are doing so in the company of a huge number of others all over the world.

And while we're about it, let's raise the stakes some more! We are actually united with the heavenly community too, whose delight it is constantly to praise God and to enjoy his presence. If we sometimes feel we are just the faithful few running the spiritual race down in the arena, remember that the stadium is packed with countless numbers of the saints cheering us on. Prayer is always a corporate activity, and our own prayer is only a tiny chirrup in the vast chorus of praise and intercession filling the heavens.

This is one of the things religious communities remind us of. Monks and nuns pray together for the world and on behalf of the world, and in a sense provide the rest of us with a tremendous cushion of prayer underlying all we do. They gather together maybe six or seven times a day simply to pray. They do scores of other things in offering hospi- tality, refuge and spiritual counsel, but essentially their work is prayer. That's what they do. And they do it together.

There's a basic lesson here. Christians who try to fly solo usually crash. They set off to storm the heavenly places by themselves but usually come spiralling down, burned by the sun and by their own spiritual pride. Christianity has always known that we need each other for this long and perilous journey, and that we need to be accountable to each other. So from the earliest times,

Christians have gathered together in communities, first in the deserts of North Africa, then in the monasteries founded under the inspiration of St Benedict, then later in various spin-off communities such as the Cistercians and Franciscans, and in our own day in new communities exploring a contemporary expression of community life, such as at Iona and Taizé.

And of course the most common form of Christian community, covering every part of the globe, is the local church – that place where the values of the kingdom of God are tested daily. This is where we can learn the importance of prayer, and the first rule of the spiritual journey – that we travel *together*.

KEY QUESTION

Do you think of yourself as an individual believer who sometimes joins other individual believers, or as a member of a family of believers, sometimes operating alone?

TRY THIS

- The staple spiritual diet of religious communities is their common prayer, called a 'daily office'. The Anglican services of Morning and Evening Prayer are a residual form of the seven daily services of monastic communities. Try using a form of daily office for at least two weeks (re-read Section 8, 'How to use a special time of prayer'). You need time to get into the rhythm of such a service and

to appreciate its strengths, one of which is the knowledge that you are praying along with countless other people using just those readings and prayers that day.

- Ask yourself the following questions about your own church:

  1 What is the 'prayer culture' of this church – how do people pray?

  2 Where is the spiritual heart of the church – where is the serious praying going on?

  Then join in! (It may be helpful to ask the priest/minister those questions too.)

- Help your local church to take its praying as a community more seriously by, for example, encouraging some of the following. These are not for you to do alone but you could ask questions about them, encourage others to do them, and offer your help. Your church could:

  1 Start a prayer group – one hour maximum, imaginatively led, varied, expectant.

  2 Take more risks with intercession in worship (see Resources), and offer training.

  3 Have short series of groups on finding Christ in silent prayer, or prayer for social justice, or prayer using the creative arts (see Section 19).

  4 Set up a 'prayer chain' so that when a prayer need arises, the chain is activated and one person phones the next on the list, until all are corporately involved.

  5 Set up a prayer room in the church, hall or elsewhere, for a week or for

Lent, where there are loads of
resources to help people pray – things
of beauty, icons, prayer stools,
books, art materials. Have this as a
'drop-in centre' for prayer.
6 Set up evening services using
different forms of prayer – Taizé,
Iona, charismatic, 'alternative
worship' – maybe using different
nights of the week. People are crying
out for worship with more creativity
and imagination, and Sunday isn't the
only night people might want to go.
7 Try a 'prayer audit' in church
asking basic questions about what
people want to help them to pray. At
its simplest this can be done in a
service with a card, one side of
which is for people to write how the
church helps them in their praying at
present, and the other side for what
they would like the church to do to
offer more help.

STORY

Old George hadn't been seen in church
for a few weeks, and one cold night
he had a visit from the minister. The
minister came in and sat himself down in
the chair by the fire opposite George.
The minister was a man of few words
and on this occasion he had even fewer.
They sat for a while in silence, and then
the minister leant forward and, using
a pair of fire tongs, picked up a piece of
burning coal from the fire and placed
it carefully in the fireplace. Together
they watched the coal sputter, smoulder

and eventually die. Nothing was said.
Then the minister said he must be
going and he left. George was back in
church next Sunday.

St Benedict

Benedict is the father of western monastic life. He was born in Italy about
480, the son of a wealthy landowner.
He went to Rome to complete his
studies but was appalled at the excesses
of life in the city and left to pursue a
monastic life at Subiaco, 40 miles east
of Rome. As he began to formulate his
ideas on how best to organize the daily
life of a monk, he decided to establish
some monasteries nearby to test these
ideas out. He established 12 communities, with 12 monks in each, under the
fatherly authority of an abbot.

This organized approach to community life was a challenge to many people
because monks had often wandered
freely and with much individual
liberty as to how they lived. After
some local opposition Benedict moved
to an abandoned pagan temple on a
mountaintop at Monte Cassino and
here built the monastery that still acts
today as the centre of the worldwide
Benedictine family.

It was here that he wrote what he
called a 'little rule for beginners', which
was actually to become the most influential blueprint for monastic life in
Europe. The Rule of St Benedict rejected
the excesses of ascetics and solitary
monks and called for communities of

enlightened self-discipline where a communal life of poverty, chastity and obedience could be lived out in an exacting but humane way. The monastic day was to be one of prayer several times together in chapel, communal meals, reading in the cloister, work in the grounds, hospitality and acts of charity. It engaged the monks' spiritual, intellectual and physical attributes, and has been found ever since to offer the most balanced and attractive model for monastic life.

Benedict died about AD 550 but he had given the West the great gift of organized monasticism, and the lessons for corporate Christian living are still essential for local Christian communities and churches today.

PRAYER OF ST BENEDICT

O gracious and holy Father,
give us wisdom to perceive you,
intelligence to understand you,
diligence to seek you,
patience to wait for you,
eyes to behold you,
a heart to meditate upon you,
and a life to proclaim you,
through the power of the Spirit
of our Lord Jesus Christ.

The Revd 'Buster' Legg boosted church attendance
with his wit and charm

14 HOW TO PRAY WITH THE EMOTIONS – THE FRANCISCAN WAY

It's funny how worried people get when they think some expression of religion is becoming 'too emotional'. And this in a culture where it's considered normal to spend an afternoon on a football terrace yelling like a five-year-old, and pledging next week's salary to the dogs' home if only the gods of football will let your team score a goal!

Emotion is a normal and necessary part of being human, but, as has been said, 'the British seem to like to go to church like they go to the bathroom, with no fuss and with no explanation if they can help it'. Some congregations seem to frown at anyone being moved by the worship, or becoming enthusiastic, or – worst of all – laughing. But what's going on here? Is God so grim that he's forgotten why he created us with a sense of humour? Would the Creator of the duck-billed platypus and the three-toed sloth be offended if we smiled with warm pleasure at his witty ideas?

I was once talking with a friend about the quality we most value in Christian people and we decided it had to be *passion*. If people are passionate about their faith then the fire is still burning and God is still let loose in their lives. But if they have become lukewarm, 'moderation-in-all-things' kind of Christians, there's a real danger that the divine tiger has been put in a cage and left in the garden.

Francis of Assisi was one of the world's passionate Christians. Whether he was responding to the beauty of nature, or to the love of Christ, or to the needs of a poor beggar, he did it with everything he'd got. Francis threw himself into everything; indeed, sometimes he pushed himself too far. But he knew it was better to go down in flames trying to give everything for everything, rather than to rust out with disuse, giving nothing for nothing.

In particular, Francis responded to wonder and love. All of us on occasion are caught out by wonder, stopped momentarily in our tracks by a sun-drenched meadow, a distant mountain peak, a playful puppy or a bluebell wood. But some of us rush on, in blind agreement with the lemmings ('there are so many of us, we must be going somewhere'), failing to notice anything that's really going on around us. And some of us try to bottle special experiences and sell them to everyone else ('come round and see our video').

But some of us will try to stop in wonder and praise to honour the moment and the Giver of it.

Elizabeth Barrett Browning had it spot on: 'Earth's crammed with heaven, and every common bush afire with God, but only he who sees takes off his shoes. The rest sit round and pluck blackberries.' Wonder is the key. Eric Liddell, the Olympic athlete whose story was told in the film *Chariots of Fire*, was being asked by his sister what he was going to do with his life. He said, 'I know that God made me for China [as a missionary], but he also made me fast, and when I run I *feel* his pleasure.' He responded to God from the depths of his being, marvelling in his gift.

The other gift that prompts our deep response is love. To know ourselves loved is to unlock a huge treasure within us which bubbles up irrepressibly throughout our lives. Francis knew himself loved as he contemplated the cross of Christ, and so deeply did he respond to that love that the stigmata – the marks of Christ's wounds – were formed on his own body. And out of that profound sense of being loved came the life of love which Francis and countless other Christians have shown to the world.

Wonder and love – two marks of a passionate faith and two wide-open doors for prayer.

KEY QUESTION

Are we afraid of our emotions getting caught up in our faith? If so, why is that a problem? Could we not 'give everything for everything' and feel the Lord's pleasure?

TRY THIS

- Let yourself be stopped in your tracks by things that take your breath away. Don't censor out the moments of wonder and amazement but pause to enjoy the experience and to thank God. It takes practice! Ask God at the start of the day to help you to *see*.
- Set a cross before you and ponder the love of God for you personally. Or ponder the words of Isaiah 43.1, 4: 'I have called you by name, you are mine ... You are precious in my sight, and honoured, and I love you.' Take your time and let those words sink into your heart.
- Try praying outdoors, and in particular by coming into close touch with the natural world. Look closely at the flowers, trees and bushes we easily take for granted. Touch and feel the physical texture of things and the life pulsing through all of nature. And be deeply thankful. Perhaps take a few items – leaves, stones, wood – and bring them to your own special place of prayer as symbols of God's generous creativity.
- You're sure to know a number of people who are hurting for all sorts of reasons – illness, bereavement, depression, frustration, mistakes made and injustices suffered. Don't take many, but take some of them with you in your imagination to the foot of the

cross, and sit down with them there. Then let things unfold in their own time ...

• At the start of your prayers, ask God for two things – absolute honesty and passionate faith. Then be honest in your prayers – express your emotions of love or anger or irritation; don't try to be a 'good Christian' who says the right things. And let your passion flow as you pray, get as deeply involved in your prayer and your concern for people as you possibly can.

QUOTE

Love all God's creation, the whole and every grain of sand in it. Love every leaf, every ray of God's light. Love the animals, love the plants, love everything. If you love everything, you will perceive the divine mystery in things. And once you perceive it, you will begin to comprehend it better every day.

Dostoevsky, The Brothers Karamazov

STORY

'Fynn, Mister God doesn't love us.' She hesitated. 'He doesn't really, you know, only people can love. I love Bossy [the cat] but Bossy don't love me. I love the pollywogs, but they don't love me. I love you, Fynn, and you love me, don't you?' I tightened my arm about her. 'You love me because you are people. I love Mister God truly, but he don't love me.'

It sounded like a death knell. 'Damn and blast,' I thought. 'Why does this have

to happen to people? Now she's lost everything.' But I was wrong. She had got both feet planted firmly on the next stepping stone.

'No,' she went on, 'no, he don't love me, not like you do, it's different, it's millions of times bigger. You see, Fynn, people can only love outside, and can only kiss outside, but Mister God can love you right inside, and Mister God can kiss you right inside, so it's different. Mister God ain't like us; we are a little bit like Mister God, but not much yet.'

Papas Fynn, Mister God, This is Anna

St Francis of Assisi

Francis was born in 1181, the son of a wealthy Italian cloth merchant. He led a fairly worldly life as a young man and was taken prisoner in a local war. After being seriously ill, he reassessed his life and was converted to a life of poverty and caring for the poor. Required to make restitution for selling some of his father's cloth for his work, Francis famously removed his own clothes in the market square and gave them back. Free of the past, he now set off on his life's work of preaching the gospel and caring for the sick.

His passionate lifestyle attracted many followers, and he found it difficult to cope with the organization of a burgeoning order of monks. He sought only to live the gospel as closely as he could to the life of Christ, and to love nature and its creatures as part of God's family. He remained a deacon all his life, but had a great respect for the Pope, bishops and clergy.

He handed over the running of the order to Brother Elias and so was free to follow his primary calling. In his last years he inaugurated the Christmas crib at Grecchio and wrote his *Testament* to add to his *First Rule* and his famous *Canticle of the Sun*. Most important of all in his latter days, however, was his being marked with the stigmata on Mount Alverna in 1224. He was ill with stomach ulcers and became blind, dying in Assisi at the age of only 45. However, his influence remains immense for the attractive wholeheartedness of his faith and his joyous response to the love of God, the natural world, and the needs of the sick and the poor.

CANTICLE OF THE SUN (EXTRACT)

Praised be thou, my Lord, with all thy creatures, especially for brother Sun, who gives the day and lightens us. And he is beautiful and radiant with great splendour: of thee, most high, he reflects the glory.

Be thou praised, my Lord, for sister Moon and the stars, in the heaven thou hast formed them, clear and precious and comely.

Be thou praised, my Lord, for brother Wind and for the air, the cloud, the serene and all kinds of weather, by which thou givest thy creatures sustenance.

Be thou praised, my Lord, for sister Water, who is very useful and humble, precious and chaste.

Be thou praised, my Lord, for brother Fire, by which thou dost illuminate the night, he is beautiful and joyful, robust and strong.

Be thou praised, my Lord, for our sister mother Earth, who sustains and rules us, and produces different fruits and coloured flowers and herbs ...

Praise and bless my Lord, give him thanks and serve him with great humility.

15 HOW TO PRAY WITH EVERYDAY LIFE – THE CELTIC WAY

There's a tendency among some people to put prayer into the Radio Three and Sunday-best category of activities. They see it as rather esoteric and probably best left to the specialists. Some graffiti on a bridge over the A1 once said: 'Prepare to meet thy God – evening dress optional.'

But anyone who has tried moving on beyond first base in prayer and Christian living will know that God is to be met in the midst of life and not just pushed out to the edges. He's a God of Wednesday morning in the rain when the car won't start, as well as Sunday morning in church when the worship has wings. If God is kept in the Victorian morning room with everyone on best behaviour, it's not surprising if our faith is dull and dutiful.

The Celts were very good at relating their faith to everyday life and activity. The Celtic Church was well embedded on the western coasts of Britain, and particularly in Ireland, long before Pope Gregory sent St Augustine to claim the land for Christ in AD 597. St Patrick (c.390–c.460) was an inspirational missionary bishop; Columba (c.521–97) took the faith into the mainland from his base in Iona; Aidan (c.600–51) presided over the strategic community at Lindisfarne; Cuthbert (d. 687) lived a saintly life and drew thousands to Christ.

The faith these men and women lived out was earthy and homely, as well as heavenly and eternal. They had prayers and liturgies for milking a cow or building a cottage or setting out on a journey. They saw God's presence woven into the very fabric of their everyday lives, and into the ebb and flow of the sea and the turning of the seasons. There was none of the modern tendency to split secular and sacred activities into separate spheres.

Prayer for us too becomes compelling and lively when we understand God to be in the thick of things throughout the day, not just waiting for us in church or in a quiet corner at home. This is a God of crowded trains and urgent meetings, of doctor's appointments and weekend barbecues, of bank statements and birthday parties. This is a God who delights in the material world – for the very good reason that he made it!

KEY QUESTION

Is your idea of God a seven-day reality, open all hours and ready for anything?

How do you relate your everyday life to him?

TRY THIS

- Use what the Celts called the *caim* – a form of prayer which encircles a person, a home, a church or anything else within the protective presence of God. It can be a very satisfying way of praying for people and situations because it has a 'physical' feel to it, as if you are really doing something significant by this prayer. 'Circle, Lord, your servant Steve with your security and confidence as he faces this interview.' 'Circle, Lord, this home with your love and fill it with your peace at this troubled time.' You might even make a circling action with your finger as you pray, as the Celts did, to emphasize it and make it real.
- Give thanks for everyday things as you encounter them during the day and pray for a good use of them, e.g. the water that pours so easily from the tap, the car that makes travel so easy, the computer that now enslaves you (!), the mobile phone that connects you from a caravan in Sussex with a daughter about to take an exam in Edinburgh (actual example!). These are everyday experiences of our material world – the equivalent of the milking of the cow and the thatching of the roof for the sixth-century Celt. Same God!
- Have as a kind of 'theme prayer' or 'prayer for the day' the following

version of the famous prayer known as 'St Patrick's Breastplate'.

Christ be with me, Christ within me
Christ behind me, Christ before me
Christ beside me, Christ to win me
Christ to comfort and restore me
Christ beneath me, Christ above me
Christ in quiet, Christ in danger
Christ in hearts of those who love me
Christ in mouth of friend and stranger.

Say this at the start of the day, 'binding' Christ to you, and the prayer will become a familiar friend, reminding you of God's presence any time you care to remember.
- Re-visit Section 7 ('How to pray through the day'), and pick up some of those ideas again.

St Cuthbert (d. 687)

Cuthbert was one of the main Celtic saints and has inspired the imagination and faith of countless Christians ever since. He was born in Northumbria and became a monk at Melrose in 651 after a vision of Aidan's soul being taken to heaven. As a missionary with a great gift for preaching he was often away from the abbey for long periods and in considerable danger, taking the gospel to the far, wild places, and seeking to bring help to needy people and to pray for them.

He became prior of the monastery at Lindisfarne but was increasingly called to solitude and the life of prayer. He would spend much time on a tiny island beside the monastery and was even known to spend the night up to his neck in the freezing water, praying. Legends grew up of his affinity with animals and birds. His preaching and pastoral care remained powerful and authentic, and it was not surprising that the king wanted him to become a bishop.

Cuthbert threw himself into his wider responsibilities, continuing to attract thousands by the way he preached and lived the gospel. However, he was desperate to return to a life of solitude and prayer and this he finally did, going to the islands of the Inner Farnes where he built a chapel and a cell, and a shelter for the many visitors who wanted to seek his wisdom. The islands are desolate but he delighted in the bird life and managed to grow some crops. However, he knew he was failing and he prepared for his death, still in his forties, but content to have been worn out for his Lord.

After a long and at times hair-raising journey around the country, his coffin eventually came to rest in Durham and the cathedral gladly and proudly gives him shelter to this day.

A CELTIC PRAYER

You Lord are in this place
Your presence fills it, your presence is peace
You Lord are in my life
Your presence fills it, your presence is peace
You Lord are in the storm
Your presence fills it, your presence is peace.
David Adam (adapted)

Markers on the way:
3 A RULE OF LIFE

The world is made up of two sorts of people: those who like shape, order and frameworks, and those who prefer to work in an open, free-ranging, spontaneous style. This section is for people who like frameworks.

Sometimes it's helpful to put this whole life of prayer and spiritual purpose into a recognizable shape, something that can act as a kind of checklist to make sure we're keeping on the move. We know how easy it is to have wonderfully good intentions but actually to drift slowly downstream and then feel too guilty to pull back the lost ground. The temptation to miss a time of prayer or Bible reading 'just this once' is all too well known by most of us, and of course, as someone said, 'the trouble with resisting temptation is that we don't want to discourage it altogether!'

So what follows is what is called a 'rule of life', which means a rule of *spiritual* life designed to guard and guide our good intentions. These are only the most general suggestions. The whole point of a rule of life is that it is personal and reasonable. No one else can impose theirs on you; your way of prayer is unique. In the old aphorism, 'Pray as you can, not as you can't.'

Worship

Maybe you decide to aim at going to church every week you're at home, and when you're away you'll go if it fits that particular situation, i.e. the friends you are with, etc.

You could decide to go to Holy Communion at least once a month, and if you've missed it, to go to a quiet mid-week Communion service instead – maybe there's a lunchtime service near where you work.

Prayer

Perhaps you decide to put aside 15 minutes a day for prayer and Bible reading Monday to Saturday, but you won't get anxious with yourself unless you miss two or three days. Guilt is a huge problem in Christian circles and we need to remember that our relationship with God is based on grace and joyful acceptance, not on regulation and duty.

You might also decide to explore the possibilities of 'chatting' prayer by using some of the suggestions in Section 7, 'How to pray through the day'.

'Ministry'

That sounds a rather grand word, but it's better than 'Church', because that suggests we're working for an institution rather than for the living God. And God is well pleased if we can offer one piece of active service for his people, whether Christian or not. So we may volunteer for the mid-week children's work or the coffee rota, standing for the local parish council or helping at the local school. God doesn't want us to become all religious and lose ourselves somewhere between the church porch and the flower store. But there are no passengers on the good ship *Body of Christ*; ministry goes with the territory if we're baptized.

Giving

If we receive without giving back or sending on, we quickly become engrossed with our own surplus fat! It's like the Dead Sea in Israel which receives fresh water from Galilee but doesn't send it on; the result is it's literally a 'dead' sea, nothing can live there. So we need to respond to the extraordinary generosity of God by giving back money, or a skill, or time, or the use of a machine or a gadget we own – the opportunities are endless.

Money is the ticklish one. People don't like to be told how much to give. But mean-spiritedness is a particular target Jesus attacks in the parables. The New Testament doesn't set a figure for giving; rather, it encourages the approach of 'sheer generosity' as exhibited in the life of Jesus. But putting that together with the Old Testament idea of the tenth, it may be that 5 per cent of income, after taxes and a roof over the head, is a reasonable target for giving to church and/or charity. That gives room for a one-off gift of spectacular generosity!

Christian growth

'To live is to change, and to become perfect is to have changed often,' said the famous Cardinal Newman. If we are to be more effective in our living for God then we'll have to commit ourselves to growing and changing, and not being satisfied with yesterday's faith. Maybe you could commit yourself to reading three or four Christian books in the year, or going on one course at church or beyond, or going to a Christian teaching and holiday week like Spring Harvest, or even investigating a certificate or diploma in Christian ministry or religious studies. Or you could commit to regular Bible reading, with notes to help (go to your local Christian bookshop for examples).

You might also consider having a spiritual friend to accompany your journey. You might arrange to see that person perhaps three or four times a year. It makes you accountable and gives you a safe place to say anything about anyone – especially yourself!

Retreats and quiet days

These may sound like luxuries for the super-pious or those with too much time on their hands. But it's not so. An annual two or three days away to think, pray, read and be gentle with yourself is an essential part of many people's journey. Your minister can advise on places. Similarly, a couple of quiet days a year can sort out jangled spiritual nerves. Ask others where they go for quiet, and if nothing else, go to a friend's spare room. As for what to do on these occasions, you could get some ideas from several parts of this book, especially Section 17, 'How to soak in silence', and Markers on the Way: 4 'Sacred times and sacred places'.

Other disciplines

You may not like the word 'discipline' but that's a cultural thing. The reality is that we all need some guidance if we're going to thrive, and discipline is just a more deliberate form of self-guidance. Here you might bring in some other aid for your spiritual journey, which could be keeping a spiritual journal, or organizing an annual fund-raising bonanza, or even taking regular physical exercise – which is part of being a whole and fully functioning person.

I hope you see what I mean by a 'rule of life'. It's entirely personal, and should be hard enough to stretch you but not so hard as to discourage you. The analogy with physical exercise is obvious.

Three final suggestions:

- Write your rule down – it's harder to cheat!
- Review it every year.
- Don't even try it if it feels like a set of regulations.

PART FOUR: PRAYING WITH ALL WE'VE GOT

16 HOW TO PRAY WITH THE IMAGINATION

The biggest obstacle to people becoming Christians in our day may not be problems of belief but pure boredom. We live in an exciting age. The possibilities of human ingenuity and technology seem to be boundless. Communication through the world wide web, WAPs, text messaging, video conferencing and the like, has reduced the world to domestic proportions while at the same time opening it up to be available as never before. The new commodity is information, and the new poverty is to be computer illiterate.

And somehow within this revolution the Church seems to belong to another world and to be wedded to another age. The way back may be to recover the primacy of the imagination as the driver of change and the way to God. The greatest human achievements are above all feats of the imagination before they're feats of engineering, quantum physics or biology. Canterbury Cathedral, relativity theory and cyberspace are all the products of supremely gifted imaginations.

This is the imagination we need to be bringing to our life of prayer. Nothing kills holiness and love more quickly than dull duty, and our life of prayer should have more in common with poetic, artistic and scientific creativity than with the demands of religious legalism. Some of our church life has about it the stale taste of the past and the requirements of conventional religion, when society is asking us for creative – even daring – presentations of the spiritual reality we have encountered in Jesus Christ.

So with our prayer – what we need to feed on and to offer to a hungry world is a spirituality which reflects our wholeness. We need a life of prayer which depends on the right-hand side of the brain as well as the left – in other words, which is open to the intuitive, creative, instinctive and artistic side of us as well as the rational, logical and ordered side. The right-hand side of the brain may be risky because it depends on imagination, story, poetry, drama, art, play, humour and the like, but it may be our last chance to make contact with a culture that's fast forgetting the Christian story.

KEY QUESTION

Will you trust your imagination, intuition and creativity as a guide on the spiritual journey? Will you pray and think 'out of the box' of conventional spiritual practice?

TRY THIS

- Water is a very powerful symbol of God's presence and love – remember the spring of water bubbling up to eternal life (John 4.14) and the river of the water of life flowing through the middle of the heavenly city (Revelation 22.1, 2). Try drinking a glass of water slowly and prayerfully, as receiving the life and Spirit of God. Or place a stone, representing your own life, in a bowl of pure, clear water, thus placing yourself in the cleansing, healing love of God. Or go and pray by a fountain or a stream, listening to and enjoying the refreshing life of Christ bubbling up within you.

- When you want to confess something you've messed up, take a stone, with all its hardness and sharp edges, and identify your mess with that stone. Feel it, know it, recognize the reality and obduracy of the mess. Then place the stone at the base of a cross, ask for forgiveness, wait long enough to receive it, and then walk away.

- St Teresa of Avila had a simple, powerful way of praying that I've known to be very moving for those encountering it for the first time. Settle down, relax, remember the presence of God. And then simply let Jesus Christ look at you *lovingly* and *humbly*. Lovingly, we might just about manage, but how can we let him look at us *humbly*? And yet is this not the God who washes feet?

Perhaps part of our own spiritual growth is to be able to let him kneel before *us*.

- Find a hazelnut (or other nut or seed) and let it be the focus of a time of meditation based on the reflections of Mother Julian of Norwich, a famous fourteenth-century mystic who wrote this:

God showed me in my palm a little thing round as a ball about the size of a hazelnut. I looked at it with the eye of my understanding and asked myself: 'What is this thing?' And I was answered: 'It is everything that is created.' I wondered how it could survive since it seemed so little it could suddenly disintegrate into nothing. The answer came: 'It endures and ever will endure, because God loves it.' And so everything has its being because of God's love.

Savour that thought as you hold the hazelnut and become more aware of the depth and seriousness of God's love for you. Then pocket the hazelnut and set off for the day!

- Candles are very productive aids to prayer. They can be lit at the start of a time of prayer and used as a reminder of the vulnerable but irresistible light of Christ burning for ever in the midst of his world. Or a candle can be lit at the start of a church meeting as a reminder, in tense moments, of the presence of Christ! If we are praying more deeply for a few people it can be helpful to light a new candle for each one as we pray for them. If we are meditating on the passion and death of Christ we can read through the passion narrative with 13 candles alight, extinguishing one candle after another as the disciples leave or betray him. Eventually only the light of Christ is left, and then – 'it is finished'. Experience the darkness.

- Get hold of Anthony de Mello's influential book *Sadhana* (see Resources section), and use some of the 50 imaginative ideas for meditation.

The labyrinth

Labyrinths were used in many medieval cathedrals, marked out on the floor, as an aid to prayer and contemplation. A very good example is to be found in Chartres Cathedral in northern France and there are signs of a renewed interest in our own day. People walk slowly along the path of the labyrinth as a form of reflective prayer, or as a very condensed form of pilgrimage. The journey is towards the centre of the labyrinth and then out again, symbolizing our moving towards God and then out again to make his presence real in his world.

It's possible to make a labyrinth in a large enough space in a church by using masking tape. Different things can be encountered on the journey through the labyrinth to help pilgrims pause, reflect and pray. A mirror – look into it and remember you are made in the image of God and you are unique. A candle – what has illuminated your way recently? Sticky notelets – who or what do you want to pray for along the way? Stones – what are the burdens that you're carrying and where can you leave them? A map and compass – what is your 'true north' and what drags you off course? At the centre – bread and wine, the presence of Christ.

With some imagination, a group of people, young and old, could work on this together and offer it as a special pilgrimage, quiet day or Lenten experience for the church.

STORY

A vicar was called in to visit an old man who was dying. They talked of many things, including how to pray. The vicar recommended the man just talk to Jesus as he would to a friend sitting at his bedside. A few days later the vicar had a phone call from the man's daughter to say that her father had died. He went round and the daughter took him to the bedroom where her father had been. 'It's strange,' she said, 'but when we found him there was a chair drawn up right alongside his bed, and Dad's head was just resting on the seat, as if it was resting in someone's lap.'

PRAYER

O Pearl of great price,
heaven cannot hold you,
yet you choose to dwell in us.

Make us worthy of such great love.
Work on the grit and dirt of our life
with your patient grace

until you have absorbed and transformed us
and your new creation is complete.

Debbie Peatman

17 HOW TO SOAK IN SILENCE

For many people there comes a time in their spiritual journey where they find themselves longing for more silence. They find a small pool of silence in the midst of a busy day and they jump in fully clothed. During prayers in the morning service they're allowed 30 seconds of silence and they fall around the neck of the person leading the prayers weeping with joy. Silence is so rare, and yet for many people today it's like a deep thirst.

Just as this page you're reading needs both black print and white paper in order for us to communicate, so in prayer we need both the 'black space' of words and the 'white space' of silence. Silence provides the context in which words may or may not be necessary. We sometimes need to sound-proof the heart in order to hear the whisper of God in a noisy world.

Silence seems to be pretty important to God. The birth of Jesus took place in the silence of a stable at night. The death of Jesus took place in the silence and darkness of a cross. The resurrection of Jesus took place in the silence before the dawn. Three huge events that took place in silence.

So we shouldn't be surprised that some of the deepest exchanges between us and God may take place in silence. If we have felt ourselves drawn to explore silence we'll need a quiet place and sufficient time. We may only start with five or ten minutes, and even that may seem agonizingly long at first, but the golden rule is 'don't panic!' Stay in there and soon that time will seem hopelessly short. It may still be difficult to stay focused, but that time will become an essential spiritual bath in which to soak and be refreshed.

Taking the water image further, what we are trying to do in silent prayer is a bit like getting under the surface of the sea where, a few feet beneath the turbulence of the waves, is a gentle stillness. Like the waves in a stormy sea, our lives may be frenetic on the surface, but underneath we may be able to enter a realm of mental and spiritual peace where our agitations are resolved and God is able to steal into our lives.

In this kind of prayer we aren't trying

to *achieve* anything. There's nothing to 'get through'. We simply open ourselves to God and wait. Certainly there are things to help us (see 'Try this'), but the essence of it is the waiting on God, listening to the silent thunder of the Lord of glory. Many times we'll walk away and not be sure what happened, if anything. But that's fine. It's the same with most evening meals in my life – I don't remember precisely what I ate last week, let alone ten years ago. But without them, and without silent prayer, my life and health would be infinitely poorer!

KEY QUESTION

Do you feel drawn to be quieter with God? When you encounter silence do you find it's becoming less of a threat and more of an invitation?

TRY THIS

Here is a three-stage approach to using silence – centring, focusing, waiting.

- *Centring.* Light a candle and watch its flickering flame. Still the body, relax the shoulders, and let the tension seep away from wherever it's located in you. (In my case it's often around the eyes and shoulders.) Don't rush this process. Body and spirit are intimately related and we need to have the body alert but relaxed. A prayer stool offers a good basis, but so too can a (not too soft!) easy chair. We don't need to take up difficult physical postures for meditation but we need

to be at home with our body. Then try imagining that you are going slowly down in a lift, descending to a deeper level of your being. Be still.

- *Focusing.* Then take whatever short biblical verse, phrase or word you find helpful as a focus for your meditation, e.g. 'The Lord is my strength and my song and has become my salvation', 'It is no longer I who live but Christ who lives in me', or shorter phrases: 'Come Holy Spirit', 'My Lord and my God', 'Into your hands …'

- *Waiting.* Then wait, repeating the phrase slowly and lovingly whenever you need to return your focus to God. It doesn't matter how often you wander off mentally. Simply return. And listen to your heart, where God will be. Perhaps you might end your time of meditation by saying the Lord's Prayer to unite you with the whole family of God.

TRY THIS

Take the phrase from Psalm 46, 'Be still and know that I am God.' Repeat it slowly and prayerfully and be still. Then drop off the last word so that you say simply, 'Be still and know that I am.' Taste all the goodness in that phrase. Enjoy the silence and simplicity of the moment. Take time. Then drop off the last words again: 'Be still and know.' Repeat the process. Then reduce the phrase to 'Be still.' Repeat. Don't be hurried. Finally reduce the phrase to its core, 'Be …'

Distractions

When you pray, doesn't your mind drift off to the football results or the need to buy more toothpaste? And then doesn't your energy go into trying to push these distractions out of the way, because holy people don't think about tooth-paste when they pray? If so, here's what to do:

- Don't fight the distractions – they'll win. Instead, write down 'toothpaste' on a piece of paper and leave it till later.
- Turn your mind back to the words, image, candle, cross or whatever you started meditating with. If you were driving a car and started to notice the fascinating things at the side of the road, you'd soon turn back to con-centrate on the road itself – either that or you'd soon be noticing things at the side of your hospital bed! Just turn your mind back to the main thing.
- Sometimes you might recognize that some quite important things are actu-ally being brought up through your subconscious in this time of silence. The prayer is enabling these things to emerge and they need proper attention and prayer, so don't ignore them. This is God's deep work of healing and growth.

QUOTES

In silence we pray, love, listen, compose, paint, write, think, suffer. Silence prevents us from trying to possess other people, or manipulate them, or make them like us. Silence creates the conditions and opportunity for us to speak, and in silence we learn what to say and how to say it.

Michael Stancliffe

Novelist Heinrich Böll writes about a man who works in a broadcasting station, talking to a friend:

'I collect a certain kind of left-overs.'
    'What kind of left-overs?' asked Mumkoke.
    'Silences,' said Murke, 'I collect silences. When I have to cut tapes, in the places where the speakers sometimes pause for a moment – or sigh, or take a breath, or there is absolute silence – I don't throw that away, I collect it ... I splice it together and play back the tape when I'm at home in the evening. There's not much yet, I only have three minutes so far – but then people aren't silent very often.'

STORY

There was once a temple on an island which was famous for its thousand bells. Not only when people rang them but also when the wind blew, the bells would ring out their wonderful symphony. But gradually, over the centuries the island sank into the sea and the temple and its bells were lost. Legend had it that the bells rang on forever and that anyone who really listened would hear them still. So a young man who had heard this legend travelled across the oceans to hear the bells, and he sat on the shore opposite the island and listened with great devotion. But all he could hear was the sound of the sea.

Day after day he returned and listened but it was always the same – just the sound of the sea. He tried incredibly hard to block out all other sounds and just to hear bells but there was nothing. Days stretched into weeks and he became more and more disheartened until finally he decided to give up. On his last day he went back to the shore to say goodbye to the island and as he lay there in the sand he simply listened to the symphony of the sea. Soon he lost himself in that deep rhythmic sound so that he was enveloped in a profound silence.

And then, in the heart of the silence, he heard something new. It was the sound of a tiny bell, followed by another and another and another. Soon all those thousand bells were ringing out with abandon, and the young man's heart was on fire with joy.

18 HOW TO ENTER THE MYSTERY

Praying in silence may lead us into still deeper waters. We start with a verse or an image to take us into silence and to act as a touchstone if we get lost, but eventually we may find that we actually enjoy being lost! Silence can become addictive!

What we're getting into now is classically called 'contemplation'. Instead of thinking or praying with words, we now cut down our actions simply to looking; we look towards God. The nearest description, perhaps, is 'gazing'. When we look at a work of art, or at someone we love, it isn't sufficient just to glance fleetingly in that direction; we need to gaze at the image before us in order to be open to all that it (or he or she) has to offer. The delight is in the looking. Small children do this naturally. You see them completely absorbed by a few shells on a beach, or the sand running through their hands. But when they grow up ...

Contemplation is about giving attention to God. We live in a culture which neurotically encourages us to give attention to ourselves, leading us to believe that with a little more self-absorption and self-help we can achieve The Answers To All Life's Problems. In that context contemplation seems so counter-cultural as to be verging on quaint. But it also strikes many people as being hugely refreshing. It points us out of our self-preoccupation and towards the crisp fresh air and the stunning beauty of the Lord of Hosts.

Our society needs contemplatives because it needs people who can 'see'. It needs contemplative *places* because that's where the atmosphere is thinner and the world of the Spirit more visible. It needs contemplative *communities* because that's where people pray steadily, look steadily and live steadily – all in the direction of God.

But we too can experience contemplative prayer.

KEY QUESTION

As you pray in silence do you find you are using fewer and fewer words and images in your mind? Does it sometimes seem that you are just lost in looking, and maybe even that it's God who is looking at you?

TRY THIS

- How to enter the mystery beyond words and images is one of the most difficult moves to describe in the whole life of prayer. How do you teach people to fall in love? They either do or they don't. But the place to start is in that silent centring, focusing and waiting described in Section 17 ('How to soak in silence').
- We may then find that we need the words and images less; they become a bit of a blur. What we find ourselves doing is simply being with God, gazing in his direction. And that's sufficient. It may be comfortable; it may be dark

and dreary. It may be wonder-full or a trackless desert. No matter: the point is to *be there*, and simply to let God be God for once.

- There are no rules in this form of prayer, and nothing to achieve. So don't go there unless you are inexorably drawn to do so. Don't imagine that contemplation is spiritually romantic and something to slip into the next conversation with the vicar. This prayer isn't for romantics; it's for mystics.

Look out for these people

These people are commonly known as mystics, fourteenth-century English variety, or sixteenth-century Spanish variety.

Julian of Norwich. A recluse who had a series of visions which she later described and interpreted in *Revelations of Divine Love*. She focused on the passion of Christ but was clear that 'all shall be well and all shall be well and all manner of thing shall be well'.

The Cloud of Unknowing. Author unknown. Between God and us is a 'cloud of unknowing' which can only be penetrated by love. Simply offering ourselves to God in naked intent is preferable to wordy meditation.

Teresa of Avila. Reformed the Carmelite order and wrote *The Interior Castle* as a wonderful description of the spiritual journey to God as a journey from the first to the seventh room where we finally have peace and stability with God.

John of the Cross. Friend of Teresa who wrote about the negative way of detachment, a journey in the dark, by night. He wrote *The Ascent of Mount Carmel*, *The Dark Night* and other books, commentaries on his mystical poems.

STORY

Anthony Bloom, the Russian Orthodox archbishop, describes in his book *School for Prayer* how, when he was a young priest, he was asked for advice on prayer by a formidable old lady who said she'd asked everyone else and they'd all failed, so maybe as he knew nothing he might blurt out something useful! Anthony Bloom took a deep breath and suggested she went to her room after breakfast, put it straight, sat down comfortably, lit a lamp in front of her icon, and just enjoyed the room. Then she should take her knitting and for fifteen minutes she should simply 'knit before the face of God', but not say one word of prayer.

After a while the old lady came back to Anthony Bloom and said, 'It works!' She'd done what he had suggested, and really enjoyed her room, which she hadn't really appreciated for years. Then she began to knit, and she became more and more aware of the silence and the peace and the rhythm of the knitting and the ticking of the clock. 'And then I perceived that the silence was not simply an absence of noise, but that the silence had substance. It was not absence of something but presence of something. The silence had a density, a richness, and it began to pervade me. The silence around began to come and meet the silence within. At the heart of the silence there was him who is all stillness, all peace, all poise.'

QUOTE

We have lost the gift of a total personal presence which I sometimes encountered in village Africa, where an adult or even a child might enter the room and squat on the floor with no more than an occasional exchange of words after the initial greeting, while I got on with whatever I was doing, until after half an hour or so of simply being together, the visitor would get up, saying, 'I have seen you,' and go. I can imagine that people who have not outgrown such simplicity would find it quite natural to sit, silent and attentive, in the presence of God for half an hour, saying only 'I have seen you,' at the end. 'Blessed are the pure in heart; they shall see God.'

John V. Taylor

PAX

All that matters is to be at one with the living God
to be a creature in the house of the God of Life.

Like a cat asleep on a chair
at peace, in peace
and at one with the master of the house,
with the mistress,
at home, at home in the house of the living,

*sleeping on the hearth, and yawning before
    the fire.*

*Sleeping on the hearth of the living world,
yawning at home before the fire of life
feeling the presence of the living God
like a great reassurance
a deep calm in the heart
a presence
as of a master sitting at the board
in his own and greater being,
in the house of life.*

D. H. Lawrence

PRAYER

*To be there before you, Lord, that's all.
To shut the eyes of my body,*

*To shut the eyes of my soul,
And be still and silent,
To expose myself to you who are there,
exposed to me.
To be there before you, the Eternal
    Presence.
I am willing to feel nothing, Lord
        to see nothing,
        to hear nothing.
Empty of all ideas,
    of all images.
In the darkness.
Here I am, simply,
To meet you without obstacles,
In the silence of faith,
Before you, Lord.*

Michel Quoist, Prayers of Life

19 HOW TO USE MUSIC AND THE ARTS

Prayer is a whole-person activity. We offer all that we are to all that God is, so that he can make us all that we might truly be. A particular gift to the life of prayer, therefore, is the world of beauty and creativity represented by the arts. Some people are propelled towards the divine more by music and poetry than by conventionally religious routes. They find themselves profoundly moved, spiritually overwhelmed, at the end of a performance of the Bach B minor

Mass, even though they find ordinary worship leaves them cold. They find the poignant precision of the poetry of George Herbert or T. S. Eliot moves them into divine territory, even though they are totally unmoved by a lifetime's diet of well-meant sermons.

God has many voices. Some people respond to the voice of the Bible and its witness to the great acts of God. Others respond more to the voice and taste of the sacraments and find especially in Holy

Communion that they touch the mystery at the heart of things. Others again find they are drawn by the voice of music and poetry, of art and sculpture. It doesn't really matter which door people come in by; it matters only that once we've made an entry, we begin to explore the whole palace we have entered.

Music and the arts, of course, have often had religion as their subject and inspiration. Bach's music was nearly always headed '*Soli Deo gloria*'– solely to the glory of God. Art galleries would be nearly empty of paintings before the eighteenth century if religious themes were excluded. Poets from John Milton and John Donne to William Wordsworth and Gerard Manley Hopkins have had the spiritual quest at the heart of their poetry.

And the public respond to this aesthetic route into the spiritual arena. The National Gallery was overwhelmed with the response to its 'Seeing Salvation' exhibition in the millennium year. Moreover, English cathedrals are experiencing unprecedented interest from the public, who are visiting in their millions. They come for the architecture, the history, the music, the worship, a distant sense of pilgrimage – all of which adds up to a form of spiritual or quasi-spiritual response to these astonishing buildings.

KEY QUESTION

Do you sometimes find yourself strangely moved by a painting or a piece of music? Do you find yourself suddenly intoxicated by a brilliant phrase of music or poetry? Do you see this as a threshold to the divine?

TRY THIS

- Listen to a piece of music, not in order to analyse it or to be religious about it, but simply to let it speak to you as deep talks to deep. Afterwards let the music roll around your memory for a while, and be thankful.
- Go to Evensong at a cathedral (thousands do!) and let the music, the economy of word and prayer, the theatre of it, carry you. Don't be tempted to resent the fact that it's the fifteenth evening of the month and the psalm has 73 verses! Instead rest gently in the beauty and rhythm of the service, and be carried by the river of prayer.
- Buy a CD or two carefully chosen to reflect your musical taste – which means it could be Mozart, Taizé or Spring Harvest – but buy them so you can use them either as part of your 'stilling-down' at the start of a special time of prayer, or as a treat in themselves, or in the kitchen or car for use when you need the deep refreshment of music.
- If you have a special place for prayer, have there, along with a Bible and other books of spiritual reading, etc., a book of poetry that speaks to you as well. Don't then feel bound to use your Bible or more obvious religious books all the time, but give yourself permission to experience the pleasure

of poetry that illuminates human living and slides you into joy.

- Take a hymnbook to your prayers and use the often profound reflections of hymn-writers as material for meditation. One man's meat is another man's embarrassment, of course, but I will gladly put my hand up to being moved and helped by the words of 'Take my life and let it be consecrated, Lord, to thee', 'When I survey the wondrous cross', 'Be thou my vision', 'Lord, for the years thy love has kept and guided', 'I, the Lord of sea and sky' and many others. Some of your favourites you might wish to photocopy and mount on card for more regular meditation.

- If there is an artist in you – however unrecognized by the exhibition-going public – you might like to treat some of your painting as a prayerful activity. Painting and prayer courses have become popular because of the common ground of attention, patience, precision, reflection, experimentation and risk, as well as the more obvious sharing of the divine attribute of creativity.

- Try responding to a Bible passage, prayer or act of worship by working with modelling clay. It can be very

Mrs Donovan could make up new hymn tunes on the spot, and sometimes did.

interesting and moving to see what comes out of the close dialogue between our creativity and that clay. We've left words behind and the spiritual imagination is able to cook up some lovely surprises!

- Icons need a whole book to themselves – indeed, there are many such books around as more and more people in the west are discovering the beauty and depth of the spirituality surrounding icons. We look *through* an icon, not *at* it. We are not to interpret but to receive. Deep thoughts may come up from the heart, but again they must be allowed to play and be themselves, and not be subjected to our instinct to analyse. All we are

doing is looking, and maybe catching the earthly end of an eternal mystery. Just look.

QUOTE

The book or music in which we thought the beauty was located will betray us if we trust to them: it was not *in* them, it only came *through* them, and what came through them was longing ... They are not the thing itself; they are only the scent of a flower we have not found, the echo of a tune we have not heard, news from a country we have never yet visited.

Evelyn Waugh

20 HOW TO PRAY IN CHURCH

Isn't it odd that one of the most difficult places to pray is in a church service? Of course, prayers are said – lots of them, and some of them by us – but overall it seems that praying in services is not hugely rewarding for many people. There are distractions – the hum on the loudspeaker system, the strange ideas of the person leading the prayers, the nagging doubt about whether we remembered to set the timer on the oven. But more than that, there's a strange distance that gets set up

between ourselves and the reality of our praying.

Why is this? For one thing, we're not on our own ground; we're trying to find common ground with everybody else and the kind of prayer used in public worship may not immediately appeal to us. For another, church services carry a lot of unspoken messages, and the atmosphere may be too full of other things for us to make contact with God for ourselves. And again, we're likely to have some responsibilities in church, at the very least for meeting and talking to fellow worshippers, and that may put us off our spiritual stride.

What can we do? The essential first move is to orientate our hearts in the direction of God in clear expectation that he is around and we can meet him in some way or other. Lack of expectancy is one of the main obstacles to a lively encounter with God. He, after all, is always hanging around, almost embarrassingly undiscriminating in his availability! It's we who don't really expect to see him there – as if the wedding guests somehow don't expect to meet the bridegroom and keep on looking past him, while asking all the time when he'll turn up.

There's a lovely challenge in a book by Annie Dillard called *Pilgrim at Tinker's Creek* in which she compares the low expectations we seem to have of an encounter with God in worship with the high-octane, fuel-injected experience it should be. She writes:

> *Why do we people in churches seem like cheerful tourists on a packaged tour of the Absolute? Does anyone have the slightest idea of what sort of power we so blithely invoke? Or, as I suspect, does no-one believe a word of it? The churches are like children playing on the floor with their chemistry sets, mixing up a batch of TNT to kill a Sunday morning. It is madness to wear straw hats to church; we should all be wearing crash helmets. [Sidesmen] should issue life-preservers and signal flares; they should lash us to our pews ...*

She exaggerates to make her point, but the truth is this: we need to come to church longing and looking for God, expecting to meet him, ears straining for the sound, on tiptoe for a glimpse. We can be absolutely sure that he's there waiting for us.

KEY QUESTION

When did you last go to worship expecting to be blown out of the water by the power and the glory (or the love and the kindness) of God?

TRY THIS

- Prepare before you go. Don't just wander in at the last moment, arriving in God's presence with hands in pockets, casually whistling a Bach chorale. As you get up in the morning, or as you walk or drive to church, or (best of all) as you sit quietly for a while the night before, call to mind what you are coming to do and who you are coming to meet. And pray for everyone involved in the worship and everyone who'll come, that the crash helmets and life-preservers will be enough to keep them safe in this great encounter with the living God!
- Make it your responsibility to pray through the service, rather than expecting others to come and 'entertain' you with their prayers. (Worship can easily become another form of entertainment in a culture where even the TV news is seen as

leisure interest.) Then pray actively before the service, before the readings, through the words of the hymns and songs, for the preacher as he or she starts up, at the end when people are going to meet over coffee or head for home. Pray with purpose, and know that you are heard. (For further ideas on this see my *Beginning Again*, SPCK 2000, pp. 68–70.)

- Have you ever gone to pray in a church during the week when there's no one else there? These sacred places where 'prayer has been made valid' are wonderful oases for us; indeed, increasing numbers of people who wouldn't call themselves Christians but know their need of holy space, are using our churches in this way – if, of course, the church is open! That's a problem in these days when churches are often damaged or despoiled if they're left open. But search out the open ones, or talk to the vicar about ways of keeping the local church open, and then drop in regularly to ponder, pray and dream.
- If you have any influence over the local church make sure the place is used to its spiritual potential. For example, have a stand with small candles which people can buy and light in order to mark their prayer, leaving the candle offering the prayer after they have left. This is extremely popular in cathedrals and many other churches today. It connects with a deep association people make between candles and prayer. Or again, try to get your church to have a board

for sticky notelets on which people can write their prayers, which the church must then offer to God at appropriate times. Or again, perhaps for a season your church could have a chapel or a room available with loads of resources for prayer – prayer stools, candles, icons, flowers, Bibles, books of prayers and on prayer, poetry, clay for creative prayerful play, and so on. Such a resource, open all day, would be likely to be very popular – especially with young mothers who have few other opportunities to develop their life of prayer except when the children are at playgroup or nursery for a few hours.

QUOTE

We ask for silver, and he longs to give us gold.

Martin Luther

A few warnings!

It's interesting how many pitfalls people fall into when praying in public! For example:

- If you go to a Prayer Breakfast in Washington DC you may find yourself in important company, so you get given a card of prayers, one of which says: 'Lord, grant that we shall not be so overawed by the presence of the President of the United States of America, that we forget thy presence.'

I'm sure the Lord will be grateful he won't be overshadowed!

- There are churches where the prayers are liberally coated with the fairly meaningless word 'just'. 'Lord, we just praise you this morning that ...'; 'Lord, we just ask you to touch the life of ...'; 'Lord, we just claim your presence now ...' It may just help the Lord just to know just how re-laxed we feel with him. But only just!

- I had recently been ordained and was praying in a group before our weekly Shoppers' Service in the Bull Ring in Birmingham. Thinking about the closeness of the busy market stalls to our church I found myself praying about the 'anomalous juxtaposition' of the two. The group said 'Pardon?'

- A vicar's daughter saw her father praying in church before he went up to preach. 'What's Daddy doing?' she whispered to her mother. 'He's asking God to help him,' came the reply. A pause while the little girl thought about this. 'Then why doesn't God help him?' she asked.

Miss Jones tried to enliven the
Litany with a Mexican wave.

Markers on the way:
4 SACRED TIMES AND SACRED PLACES

Derek Draper, young, successful, upwardly mobile former parliamentary lobbyist, wrote this:

> *Next to Westminster Abbey there's a beautiful little church. In five years of working in Parliament I don't think I had ever really noticed it. I went in. I gazed at the altar for a moment and then lowered my head and closed my eyes. Instantly I became conscious of how quiet the church was. I breathed deeply and, to my amazement, I started to have the same feelings I had when doing yoga – a sense of my non-physical self unfolding, stretching out, being at peace. It occurred to me that maybe I was feeling what people call the presence of God. I don't suppose I knew what 'prayer' really was, so I found myself reciting the Lord's Prayer, remembered from two decades earlier. Then I found prayer coming so naturally that I felt as you do when you wake from a nightmare and momentarily cannot breathe, then suddenly take a great gulp of air. Released. Heard.*

What I take from this is the importance of special places. Places where, as T. S. Eliot said, 'prayer has been valid'. When we enter these places they speak directly to our hearts and bring people to silence and the threshold of prayer. We probably have our own local places which are special, be they a corner of a church, a tree in a field, a hill overlooking the town, or a bench by the river.

However, there are also places which have been able to hold and nurture the special experiences of many people over a long time. These are places which begin to acquire the adjective 'sacred'. There's a depth to them, a sense of presence, a holiness. And these are the places to which people start coming as pilgrims. There are many hundreds of places around the world which have this power of unselfconscious attraction, but the ones that follow are some of

the most popular among people from Britain.

Taizé. An ecumenical community in Burgundy founded by Brother Roger in the Second World War, and now drawing hundreds of thousands of young people from all over Europe by the power of its witness among the poor and by the haunting quality of its music.

Iona. Another ecumenical community, founded by George MacLeod in the 1930s on the small Scottish island from which Columba had staged his mission in the sixth century. Today the community is noted for its social commitment, its music and its innovative liturgies.

Santiago de Compostela. Great numbers go to this city in north-west Spain, supposedly the burial site of St James. Pilgrimage routes to Compostela are to be found all over Europe and the traditional pilgrim badge of a scallop shell originated here.

Lindisfarne. This Northumbrian island (also called Holy Island) is particularly associated with the great seventh-century bishop, St Cuthbert, whose holiness led to many stories and much devotion. Lindisfarne is cut off by the high tide and retains an aura of sanctity, especially when the crowds have gone home!

Canterbury. This was the greatest centre of pilgrimage in Britain for many centuries, based on the stirring martyrdom of Thomas Becket in 1170. The shrine was destroyed by Henry VIII, but today a million visitors a year come to this holy place, which is also the symbolic centre of the Anglican Communion.

Other great centres of pilgrimage are to be found in every continent (and every religion), for example, **Walsingham, Assisi, Lourdes, Our Lady of Guadalupe,** as well, of course, as **Rome** and **Jerusalem.**

AN INCIDENT

I was walking through the cloisters at Canterbury when I saw a man sitting there looking pensive. I asked him if he'd been to Canterbury before. 'Yes,' he said, 'I was here eleven years ago and this place saved my life. I was in a very bad way – and this place really saved my life.' I didn't ask why. What he'd told me was enough.

THE PILGRIMS' SONG

So brethren, let us sing alleluia now. Sing as travellers sing along the road, but keep on walking. Sing, but keep on walking. What do I mean by walking? I mean press on from good to better. Paul says there are some who go from bad to worse. But if you press on, then you keep on walking. So sing alleluia, and keep on walking.

St Augustine

A STORY ABOUT SEARCHING

A man found his friend on the ground under a street lamp, searching for his keys. He joined in the search but they had no luck. Eventually the man said, 'Where did you lose the keys?' 'At home,' said the friend. 'Then why are you searching here?' asked the man.

'Because the light is brighter here,' said his friend.

Search for God where he's likely to be found, not where the lights are brightest.

A PRAYER FOR PILGRIMAGE

Pilgrim God, bless us with courage where our way is fraught with danger

Bless us with good companions, where the way demands a common cause

Bless us with good humour, for we cannot travel lightly when weighed down with too much solemnity

Bless us with humility, to learn from those around us

Bless us with decisiveness, when we have to move quickly

Bless our lazy moments, when we need to stretch our limbs for the journey

Bless us, lead us, love us and bring us home, bearing the gospel of life. Amen.

PART FIVE: DARKNESS AND LIGHT

21 HOW TO PRAY IN BAD TIMES

I came to a grinding halt in the summer of 1979. Utterly spent after a huge youth event I'd been organizing, my body decided to throw all the alarm switches and red lights were flashing everywhere. It was complete nervous exhaustion. Fortunately I had a wise Christian doctor. She gave me a way of understanding what was going on; she got me to stop; and she got me to refill my spiritual reservoir. I now even find I'm grateful for the experience.

But one thing I couldn't do was pray in any of my normal ways. Prayer didn't touch it. I was wiped out, and so were conventional ways of praying. That's what many people find when bad times come rolling down the mountain and envelop them in darkness. No trite 'God'll-fix-it' prayer, no well-meaning 'We'll pray for you', no 'You'll be better soon' can cope with the bewilderment and panic. This is when we need to dig deeper.

When serious illness turns a summer day into an arctic night; when a core relationship falls apart; when a teenage child isn't just going off the rails but leaving the entire rail network; when we're on the ropes like that, we need prayer that's 'been there', that's stood alone in the darkness. And at that moment we might rediscover the psalms.

All human life is depicted in the psalms, the prayer book of the Jews. In them we find the whole range of emotion from terrible vindictiveness to wild delight, from aching despair to passionate desire. Count the number of powerful emotions in Psalm 55, for example. Feel the sense of isolation in Psalm 142, the sense of rejection (and trust) in Psalm 31, the despair because of illness and guilt in Psalm 38. And have a large whisky before you tackle Psalm 58!

These are prayers to accompany us through bad times – thoroughly honest, sparing nothing. We may take issue with some of the theology that seems to blame God for sending ailments but the sheer audacity and searing humanity of these prayers is breathtaking.

It's companions like these that we need when our world is falling apart. We need friends in low places, people who have entered the darkness and spoken quietly of how they survived. A nun wrote of her time in Chile when disaster came calling and she likened it to the invasion of a flood;

And I knew that there was neither flight
nor death nor drowning
That when the sea comes calling you stop
being good neighbours,
Well acquainted, friendly-from-a-
distance neighbours
And you give your house for a coral castle
And you learn to breathe under water.
                                    Carol Bialock

Learning to breathe under water is the task. Learning to draw on the wisdom of others with a story to tell. Learning most of all from a man who hung on a dark cross and experienced even the abandonment of God.

KEY QUESTION

Who would I trust enough to let them share my times of greatest trial? And where in the Bible have people 'been there' in the dark – and come back?

TRY THIS

- Read Psalm 73. It's a plea for relief from oppressors of some kind but the 'oppressors' can be used as a symbol for whatever experience it is that's oppressing us, be it illness, anxiety, failure, depression. Verses 1 and 2 state the problem. Verses 3–12 show how the 'oppression' succeeds and prospers. But then we see that those evils will ultimately fail (vv. 16–20), and that becoming embittered will have the effect of cutting us off from God too (vv. 21–2), and finally that despite everything God is and always will be with us (vv. 23–8). Here in this psalm is both protest and intimacy – a good model for praying in bad times.
- Other psalms can function in this way: Psalm 69 when we are feeling persecuted or on trial, Psalm 77 when we feel alone and rejected, Psalm 51 when we are weighed down with having made a mess of things, Psalm 6 when serious illness is around. Remember that the enemies who often feature in the psalms can be used as symbols for our own internal 'enemies', the things that undermine or assault us from within.
- The cross is the place and the motif to which our bad times can ultimately be brought. God doesn't offer cast-iron answers to the questions we have about suffering, but he enters the questions and participates in the suffering, in the life and the terrible death of Jesus. When nothing else helps, look at the cross, read the accounts in the Gospels, imagine you are there. And remember the truth that in the last resort only a suffering God can help any of us.
- Because one of the hardest things to do when you are in a really bad place is to pray, ask others to do so for you. Our natural human reserve will often hold us back from this but the knowledge that, even though you can't do it, others are holding you steadily before God, can be a huge strength. Take the risk of asking and people will be honoured to do it. Religious communities are especially valuable in this way.

QUOTES

Some of you say 'Joy is greater than sorrow', and others say, 'Nay, sorrow is the greater.' But I say to you, they are inseparable. Together they come, and when one sits alone with you at your board, remember that the other is asleep upon your bed.

Khalil Gibran

God is love and he enfoldeth
   all the world in one embrace;
with unfailing grasp he holdeth
   every child of every race.
And when human hearts are breaking
   under sorrow's iron rod,
then they find that self same aching
   deep within the heart of God.

Timothy Rees

STORY

In a concentration camp in the last war the rabbis assembled to debate whether God could exist, given the appalling experiences of the Jewish people in the camps. All afternoon they argued away, quoting the Torah and the Talmud, deeply involved in the learned debate. Eventually they decided, with great reluctance, that all the evidence pointed to the fact that God did not exist. There was a silence, and then the chief rabbi among them got up. 'Nevertheless,' he said, 'it is time for our evening prayers.' And they all got up and followed him to the place of prayer.

PRAYER

*O Lord, remember not only the men and
   women of goodwill but also those of ill
   will.
But do not only remember the suffering they
   have inflicted on us,
remember the fruits we bought thanks to this
   suffering,
our comradeship, our loyalty, our humility,
   the courage, the generosity, the greatness
   of heart which has grown out of all of this.
And when they come to the judgement let all
   the fruits that we have borne be their
   forgiveness.
Amen, amen, amen.*

*Written on a piece of wrapping paper near
the body of a dead child in Ravensbrück,
where 92,000 women and children died.*

22 HOW TO PRAY IN THE WILDERNESS

Sometimes prayer is simply boring. We don't like to admit that. Indeed, Christians have a vested interest in making it seem that our faith is successful and enjoyable, and that it works. It's understandable. Why else should anyone want to become a Christian if it doesn't work? But nevertheless, sometimes it all seems meaningless and dry. We've run out of energy. The tank is empty.

If you ask people why they are Christians you might get answers like, 'Because it gives my life meaning,' 'Because it works,' 'Because it's true.' But you then have to ask the questions: What happens when that faith doesn't make sense of what's going on in your life? What happens when it doesn't seem to work? What happens when serious doubts begin to assail the mind and gnaw away at the heart? Because they will.

Consider the experience of one leading spiritual writer, Henri Nouwen, whose books and teaching have inspired millions.

So what about my life of prayer? Do I like to pray? Do I want to pray? Do I spend time praying? Frankly, the answer is no to all three questions. After sixty-three years of life and thirty-eight years of priesthood, my prayer seems as dead as a rock ... I have paid much attention to prayer, reading about it, writing about it, visiting monasteries, and guiding many people on their spiritual journeys. By now I should be full of spiritual fire, consumed by prayer. Many people think I am and speak to me as if prayer is my greatest gift and deepest desire.

The truth is that I do not feel much, if anything, when I pray. There are no warm emotions, bodily sensations, or mental visions. None of my five senses is being touched – no special smells, no special sounds, no special sights, no special tastes, and no special movements.

Whereas for a long time the Spirit acted so clearly through my flesh, now I feel nothing. I have lived with the expectation that prayer would become easier as I grow older and closer to death. But the opposite seems to be happening. The words 'darkness' and 'dryness' seem best to describe my prayer today ...

Are the darkness and dryness of my prayer signs of God's absence, or are they signs of a presence deeper and wider than my senses can contain? Is the death of my prayer the end of my intimacy with God or the beginning of a new communion, beyond words, emotions, and bodily sensations?

Henri Nouwen, Sabbatical Journey

Unfortunately we can't answer that last question because a few months later Nouwen was dead. But it's a vital question for many people because it's part of a larger question: is this experience of dryness just a particular passing phase due to all sorts of other factors, or is it a major stage in my Christian journey?

There's an important divide here. Much spiritual dryness is due to external factors. We've been on the Christian road a long time and are just travel weary. We're tired and stressed in other areas of life and so, of course, our spiritual life reflects that. We've got stuck in a set of Christian practices of worship and prayer that we've outgrown and we need a new wardrobe. There are all sorts of reasons.

But there's another experience altogether that starts out looking the same –

boredom, listlessness, dryness – but is actually what has often been called 'the dark night of the soul' or senses. This is the experience when, as Henri Nouwen wonders, we are being moved on by God to a profounder union with the divine where we are too close to the light to see it. St John of the Cross explained it by saying that the clearer the light shines, the more it blinds and darkens the eye of the soul. The eye of the soul dilates, and faith becomes trust in the unseen God. If the experience of darkness is of this sort then God is in charge and he is teaching the Christian not to rely on the senses but on him alone. It's a stage of growth.

But if it's the other sort of darkness where we've run our truck into the desert and got stuck in the sand, then there will be things we ourselves could be doing about it. The question we are then being asked is like the question asked by the group leader in the mountains after his party has collapsed on the ground for a break: 'Shall we move on?' he asks optimistically. If we don't get up and move on with the main party, all we can do is dawdle ineffectually down the mountain, but if we're ready to move on there's new territory to explore and new height to be gained. And that's what this section is about – hearing the question 'Shall we move on?' and answering, 'Yes.'

KEY QUESTION

Are there purely circumstantial reasons why my prayer life has gone off the boil?

Am I tired, stressed, ill, moving house or changing job, depressed, having a bad patch in relationships, bereaved, on a diet, etc.? We're a unity of mind–body–spirit, and therefore each part will affect the others. Alternatively, do I just need to move on into a new way of praying?

TRY THIS

- Relax, it *will* pass.
- Look back, look forward. It may be good to look back and identify some safe places, some ways of prayer which we know are always helpful but which we've forgotten about – some pattern, or author, or idea. On the other hand it may be good to look forward as well and take a risk with some other forms of prayer which you've never thought of as 'you' but which may be where God is calling you now. What other ways of praying in this book, for example, might beckon you?
- Plod on. The Christian journey isn't all champagne and fireworks, in spite of the books and testimonies you might have read by people whose experience of the miraculous leaves you breathless and with a faint desire to take them off at the knees. Much of the Christian life isn't champagne but tea and biscuits. So keep going, pray on, stay faithful, change a bit here and there – and wait for the Lord.
- Talk to a Christian friend you instinctively respect. Ask for some of their time, and whether you could meet them every few weeks to see how

you're getting on. Finding this 'right' person may be difficult, but listen to your heart here – unexpected people may come into the frame.

- Join a home group, prayer group or some equivalent, where you can rest in the corporate faith of the group. The Christian journey was never meant to be taken alone anyway, and too much introspection can damage your spiritual health. Allow yourself to be carried for a while, but offer your gifts and insights to the group and you may begin to feel the spiritual energy seeping back.
- Be patient. We aren't machines to 'fix' and sort out, but people to heal and grow.

QUOTE

We must not come to God in order to go through a range of emotions, nor to have any mystical experience. We must just come to God in order to be in his presence, and if he chooses to make us aware of it, blessed be God, but if he chooses to make us experience his real absence, blessed be God again, because he is free to come near or not.

Anthony Bloom, Living Prayer

PRAYER

God grant me the grace to accept with
*   serenity*
the things I cannot change,
courage to change the things I can,
and wisdom to know the difference,
living one day at a time,
enjoying one moment at a time;
accepting hardship as the pathway to peace,
taking as you did this sinful world as it is,
not as I would have it;
trusting that you will make all things right,
if I surrender to your will;
that I may be reasonably happy in this life,
and supremely happy with you forever in the
*   next.*

Reinhold Niebuhr

23 HOW TO THINK THROUGH PROBLEMS

Isn't prayer a rather infantile activity?

'I mean, you grow out of it, don't you? It's nice to believe in a friendly face behind the clouds when you're young, but in the real world you make your own luck. It's tough out there and you've got to be tough yourself if you're going to survive. Prayer belongs to junior school.'

There are three things to say to all that. In the first place, it's not infantile to pray to God if in fact the human heart is made for him, if the deepest reality of our being is that we are constantly searching for our spiritual home. People of faith maintain that our deepest selves need to 'dock' with God if we are to grow towards wholeness. Prayer then becomes a sign of maturity, not of childishness.

Second, prayer can certainly be infantile if as adults we still pray in infantile ways. The fresh faith of a child can be truly delightful. Remember the prayer of a child overheard by his mother: 'Dear God, please look after Mum and Dad, and Stephen, and Grandma and Granddad, and Aunty Clare and Uncle Mark, and our dog Spot, and please look after yourself, because if you don't do that, we're all sunk!' But we grow into more thoughtful and considered forms of prayer as we grow older and more experienced in faith. Prayer may become more reflective and our requests more nuanced. Just as other relationships mature, so will our relationship with God in prayer.

Third, there's a difference between being *childish* and being *childlike*. It's not appropriate to pray in child*ish* ways when we are adults. To pray that my Lottery number will come up isn't likely to persuade the celestial civil service! It isn't really on (though it's entirely understandable) to pray as the woman did when she'd dropped a whole tray of crockery: 'Dear God, may that not just have happened!' But it certainly is appropriate for us to pray with the child*like* trust of one who knows their heavenly Father to be entirely good, compassionate and true. That's why Jesus told us that when we pray we should call God *Abba* – Dad.

How can we pray meaningfully when we live in a universe governed by scientific laws?

Well, let's clear the ground a bit here. So-called 'scientific laws' are in fact only the regularities we observe in nature.

They're not written in cosmic stone. These regularities are of course essential to us. We need to know that jumping off a cliff will have certain negative consequences. But the natural world is much more 'open-textured' than our limited understanding supposes. Scientists tell us that the deepest level of reality we can understand thus far isn't at all solid but is made up of a swirling mass of string-like energy. We know that the universe isn't predictable in the normal understanding of the word, but is built up of a subtle interplay of chance and necessity.

When we pray, therefore, we aren't throwing paper darts at some iron wall of natural law. We're co-operating with God in his massive enterprise of healing creation, bit by bit. When I pray I'm not asking God to interrupt the ordinary workings of the universe. I'm asking him to work within the created order of things so that the full potential and capacity of that part of creation may be released. I'm looking for the natural order to be at full stretch, just as it was in Jesus (which is why amazing things happened around him).

This approach to prayer therefore sees God not as *over*-ruling anything so much as *under*-ruling it. He rules from *within* his created order. God's action isn't a violation of 'natural law'; rather, it is itself the natural law of a deeper order of reality, what happens when we break through to the deepest levels of nature's operation.

Prayer then becomes an exciting co-operation with the One who holds everything in being. God doesn't have to squeeze into his world like a child trying to get into his parents' dinner party. It *is* his world and he wants to share its joys and responsibilities with us. In prayer we work at it together.

What about prayer that never gets answered?

What indeed! Who of us hasn't got a few questions to ask God when we get to meet him? What about the floods and famines we prayed about, the weeping by the bedside, the desperate praying for a wounded marriage? What more does this God want, to get him into action?

Well, if we remember the last question about a scientific universe we'll realize that God is both free and limited within the fabric of his creation. He has limited himself in the interests of love. He has tied his hands behind his back in the very act of creating a universe in order that it should have the freedom to be itself. It happens in any human act of creation, too. When we 'create' children (without going into details!) we limit our freedom over them. They have an independent existence which means that we can thereafter persuade, advise or cajole our children, but we can't enforce anything ultimately, except in the most meaningless sense. John V. Taylor once wrote: 'The truth about God is not so much that he is omnipotent as that he is inexhaustible, and for that reason he will always succeed.' But 'success' may not be as we know it!

Two people I know and care for have cancer as I write. I'm praying for them both but I know that the course of their illness will inevitably be different. What if one has a marvellous remission and the other dies rapidly? What will I say about the use of my prayer or the trustworthiness of God? What I hope I'll do is realize that God is absolutely committed to both these people and wills the very best for both of them. Indeed, he will be working flat out, within the givens of the situation, for the welfare and wholeness of both. But what I also hope I'll accept is that there are intrinsic limitations to those 'givens', and I don't know what they are. Who knows what almighty Love can do in one situation (in a universe created by Love), but who knows what impossibilities there are in another situation (in a universe where you can't have dry rain or square circles)?

Prayer is a risky venture. We don't know what will happen to those we pray for or to those of us who pray. But our responsibility is simply to pray; God's responsibility is to use our prayers. Our responsibility is to love (that's what prayer is); God's responsibility is to use that love for the good of others.

What if I never feel anything special when I pray?

Don't worry – most people don't. Indeed the opposite danger is true, that some people may work up their emotions so that they have a manufactured set of responses to prayer – usually ones that leave the rest of us feeling distinctly excluded or uncomfortable. The point to remember is that feelings are the least reliable of our criteria for meaningful prayer. Prayer is being present to the presence of God. Prayer is the gift of ourselves to God in response to the Gifts he has given to us. Prayer is listening, loving, embracing people in God. Prayer is holding open the door of opportunity in places of despair. Prayer is struggle, joy, laughter and pain. In other words, prayer doesn't have to be a spiritual massage, a scent of roses and a warm glow. It's too important for that.

What matters more than how we feel is what we bring. If we bring ourselves and the people on our hearts then we'll be entering the arena of prayer with honesty and love. What happens then is God's business. If we're taken off to the seventh heaven – wonderful (and sometimes it will happen). If we're left cleaning up the spiritual garbage – thanks be to God (someone had to do it). Some of us are more emotional than others and God works with us as he finds us. Faithfulness matters more than feelings.

On the other hand, it's important that prayer doesn't remain at the level of duty and determination all the time. As the psychotherapist Carl Jung said, 'It is of the highest importance that people should know religious truth as a thing living in the human soul, and not as an abstruse and unreasonable relic of the past.' Prayer has to permeate the heart. Nevertheless, that permeating can be done through inner conviction as well as through feelings.

Different people will experience prayer in different ways, and long live the difference!

24 HOW TO STAY FRESH

Prayer is a long-term relationship, not a one-night stand. It therefore has its moments when you say to yourself: 'Whose clever idea was this, then?' There aren't many days when we wake up thinking, 'Oh, what a beautiful morning – can't wait to pray!' We're not talking here about the spiritual wilderness of Section 22, just the ordinariness of much of the Christian journey.

A lot of the road to heaven has to be taken at 30 miles an hour. Occasionally we get on to a stretch of motorway and take off, but more often we have to go through the built-up areas, the road works and the general snarl-up of life – and in the middle of all that, to keep reasonably fresh at the wheel.

It might be helpful every so often to do a kind of spiritual audit and ask ourselves these sorts of questions:

- Does the word 'prayer' feel warm or cold to you at present?
- On a scale of 1 to 10, how well do you feel you are doing in keeping prayerfully in touch with God?
- What's at the heart of your prayer life right now?
- Do your inner and outer lives feel in touch with each other at the moment?
- What levels or types of prayer do you seem to be using these days? (see Section 5)
  1 'Just getting on with it' (but remembering God is there).
  2 Chatting (quick-contact, 'instant access' prayer).
  3 Talking (time set apart for the purpose).
  4 Intimacy (going beyond words).
- If you were to think of yourself as a 'praying animal' (which we are), what animal would you be? And why? A small black and white mongrel, well-meaning but insecure? A brown bear, crashing about in the forest in a rather ungainly fashion? A kitten, curled up in his Master's lap but sometimes stuck up a tree!

The answers to these questions may be encouraging or dispiriting. The point is not to get stressed about it but to realize that Christian living has the full range of experiences and emotions which we know in any important relationship. The task is to keep our prayer and life of faith as fresh as possible without expecting always to be living on the spiritual equivalent of cloud nine.

KEY QUESTION

Am I prepared for the long-distance running of the spiritual life – rather than the quick sprint – and am I prepared to make it one of my life's joys and struggles to commit myself to the task?

TRY THIS

- Use the audit (above) every so often to check how you're getting on. In particular, examine your practice of prayer to see if you've started cutting corners and settling for minimalist prayer! Just realizing what's going on will usually be enough to make you brush off the dust and freshen up your praying.
- Focus on God, not on prayer. This is crucial. Prayer can itself become a kind of idol so that we get stuck contemplating our spiritual navel rather than contemplating God himself. The arrow of prayer becomes a boomerang of self-absorption. Try quoting often the opening verses of Psalm 42, 'As a deer longs for flowing streams, so my soul longs for you, O God. My soul thirsts for God, for the living God.' *Long* for God. *Thirst* for him.
- Occasionally re-visit some sections of this book and see if you are drawn to some different form of prayer. Even if it didn't appeal to you a while ago, the time might now be right

because we all move on. In any case, no growth in prayer is possible without some venture out of your comfort zone.

A helpful litany

(Say it with someone else, or say it to yourself; say it in all situations; say it boldly or say it quietly; say it with pleasure or say it against the odds; but say it faithfully and say it often.)

> *God is good,*
> *all of the time.*
> *All of the time,*
> *God is good.*

JOKE BOX

It was a Jewish boy's special day – his bar-mitzvah – but sadly a silver spoon went missing. Even more unfortunately, the rabbi was caught on video putting the silver spoon in his pocket, but the family decided not to do anything about it. Some years later the Jewish boy was getting married, and it was the same rabbi who was taking the service. The Jewish boy said to the rabbi, 'Rabbi, you know we saw you putting that silver spoon in your pocket at the bar-mitzvah.' 'Ah,' said the rabbi. 'Did you never find it? That's odd – I put it in your prayer shawl!'

PRAYER OF SIR FRANCIS DRAKE

O Lord God, when thou givest to thy servants to endeavour any great matter, grant us to know that it is not the beginning but the continuing of the same unto the end, until it be thoroughly finished, which yieldeth the true glory; through our Redeemer, Jesus Christ. Amen.

25 HOW TO MAKE ALL OF LIFE A PRAYER

There was a book which came out in 1963 called *Prayers of Life* by a French priest named Michel Quoist. It blew like a gale through the staid vocabulary of a lot of conventional prayer, largely because it refused to recognize any human experience as off-limits to prayer. So there are prayers over a five-pound note, a wire fence, a tractor, football at night – even a bald head! One section of the book is headed 'All of life would become prayer', and the phrase has always stuck in my mind as the final goal of all this activity we call prayer – not that all of life should be made up of religious piety, but that all of life should be gently lived before God.

Margaret Silf, in the final chapter of her book *Taste and See*, uses the illustration of a birdwatcher who sometimes goes into his hide, but who actually learns to listen to the birds all the time, not just when he goes into his special place. The birdwatcher gradually becomes tuned in to the birds *permanently,* even when he's not in his hide, and he notices all the patterns in the songs and the subtle changes in modulation and pitch, and indeed the whole panorama of sound which the rest of us usually screen out.

So our special times of prayer, our times in the 'hide', help us to tune in to the fullness of God's voice which is constantly with us, but is usually unheard against the background hiss of modern life. There is a place for effort in prayer, for the disciplines and practices throughout this book, but the ultimate goal is beyond the exercises themselves. The goal is that all of life should become prayer, lived thankfully in the presence of God.

When a human life is entirely pervaded by the presence and love of another person, he or she experiences life as a limitless possibility. Life is breathtakingly beautiful, and obstacles are there to be leapt over. So if a human life is entirely pervaded by the presence and love of God, who knows what might happen? It will certainly be good – very good. All of life will become wrapped up in the light and tenderness of God. All of life will become prayer.

KEY QUESTION

Are you prepared for this goal to be unobtainable but still worth going for? Do you mind that growth in holiness is a life-long process of opening ourselves to God, and there are no over-the-counter prescriptions? And will you keep praying until you simply can't live without it?

TRY THIS

- Persevere.
- Persevere.
- Persevere.

QUOTES

Although Christianity seems at first to be all about morality, all about duties and rules and guilt and virtue, yet it leads you on out of all that into something beyond. One has a glimpse of a country where they do not talk of those things, except perhaps as a joke. Everyone there is filled full with what we would call goodness, as a mirror is filled with light. But they do not call it goodness. They do not call it anything. They are not thinking of it. They are too busy looking at the Source from which it comes.

C. S. Lewis, Mere Christianity

Mother Julian of Norwich had a series of mystical experiences ('showings') which she meditated on for fifteen years, seeking to understand them, before writing about them in her Revelations of Divine Love. *Here is a famous passage about the goal of the spiritual journey:*

And from the time it was shown, I often asked to know what was our Lord's meaning. And fifteen years after I was answered in inward understanding, saying this:

> *Would you know your Lord's meaning in this?*
> *Learn it well.*
> *Love was his meaning.*
> *Who showed it you? Love.*
> *What did he show you? Love.*
> *Why did he show you? For love.*
> *Hold fast to this and you shall learn and know more about love, but you shall never know nor learn about anything except love, for ever.*

PRAYER

I am no longer my own, but yours.
Put me to what you will, rank me with whom you will.
Put me to doing, put me to suffering:
Let me be employed for you, or laid aside for you:
Exalted for you, or brought low for you:

Let me be full, let me be empty:
Let me have all things, let me have nothing:
I freely and wholeheartedly yield all things
To your pleasure and disposal.
And now, glorious and blessed God,
Father, Son and Holy Spirit,
You are mine and I am yours. So be it.
And the covenant now made on earth,
Let it be ratified in heaven.

The Methodist Covenant, 1755

Into your hands, Lord, we commit our
  spirit
into your hands, the open and defenceless
  hands of love,
into your hands, the accepting and
  welcoming hands of love,
into your hands, the firm and reliable hands
  of love,
we commit our spirit.

Rex Chapman

Markers on the way:
5 SETTING THE COMPASS

The time has come for the real journey to begin. This book has tried to offer a whole range of useful items to put in the rucksack, but only you can make the journey. When our daughter set off for her gap year in Africa, everything she needed for a year had to go into one rucksack, and as parents we worked hard with her to make sure she had the right things. But one morning she went through the airport departure gate alone.

The adventure of prayer is more than a year; it's a lifetime journey into God, and into the high mountains of the spirit. Although the journey is ours and no one can make it for us, nevertheless we can take a rucksack full of good things and, more importantly, we'll be travelling with the very best Guide there is – Jesus Christ himself, who promised to be with us always, to the end of all time (Matthew 28.20). That's a high level of security!

But before we can set out on any significant journey – for instance, marriage, or a career – we need to have a pretty reasonable level of self-knowledge and self-awareness, or we might just come unstuck a little way down the track. So too in the spiritual journey it's important to have some self-knowledge so that we know in broad terms what

helps us spiritually, where we can go to find nourishment.

Because human personality is so astonishingly diverse, it shouldn't be a surprise that we have different types of spirituality as well. Throughout this book there will have been things that have attracted you and other things that have elicited little more than a slightly bored 'ho-hum'. So it might now help to consider what kind of spiritual 'personality' you have, and where you can find your daily bread – or caviar.

I've found it useful to adapt a scheme of the nineteenth-century philosopher Friedrich von Hügel who wrote about various 'schools of prayer', represented by particular biblical characters. The point about the brief descriptions that follow is not to try and find a perfect match or expect only to resonate with one or other of the 'schools'. The point is

to recognize one (or two) schools which feel to be some sort of spiritual home, while probably finding attractive some part of each of the schools. Knowing our 'home' can give us confidence in our own spiritual journey and prevent us from being threatened by the strange spiritual passions of other Christians. It may come as a relief that you can be a Christian without being slain in the Spirit, contemplating candles or handling poisonous snakes!

School of St Peter

This form of spirituality shares some of the robust, 'get-on-with-it' characteristics we associate with Jesus' forthright, red-blooded friend Peter. If this is your spiritual home, you probably pray best in set forms with a recognizable structure, maybe using books of prayers to help. You're likely to be a concrete thinker, attracted to regular worship in church and the unfolding drama of the Church's year, particularly in Holy Week and Easter. You will be loyal and faithful in prayer (at least in intention!) and may value a rule of life or a spiritual friend. Holy Communion may be important to you, but you're more concerned with good, well-prepared and well-led worship. Among the Gospels, Mark may be your favourite.

School of St Paul

Paul was the thinker of the early Church, a passionate and intelligent

man with a drive to perfectionism. If you pray in this school, you will be thoughtful about prayer and worship, wanting it to make intellectual sense, to be anchored in scripture and to be related to the public world, not just to personal experience. You will probably be a regular reader of Christian books and a lively critic of sermons! You will be less attracted to what you see as superficial emotion in worship but are actually capable yourself of a deep, passionate response to God; there may be something of the mystic in you. Intercessions should be about the real world and things that matter, not just fluffy personal issues. Among the Gospels you may be drawn to Matthew or to John.

School of St John

Tradition has it that John not only had a special friendship with Jesus, he also had many years to ruminate on the events of Jesus' life and death, and these profound reflections are the core of John's Gospel. It's that reflective quality that marks this type of prayer. Prayer is more of a seeking and a reaching out, a longing. It's more opaque and more exploratory. Prayer needs time and space because essentially it's about entering a mystery, not getting a result. You may use few words but value silence, symbols, imagination, poetry. You may prefer a quiet early morning service to the mid-morning all-age jamboree, and you may be rather impatient with what you perceive as superficial prayer and worship which doesn't attend to depth and mystery. Intercession may be your least favoured form of prayer but you respond to imaginative new methods. John's Gospel has to be the one you prefer.

School of St Francis

Francis is the popular saint of today because of his obvious love of nature and of ordinary people, and because he was a man of integrity and bold action, giving to the poor and living himself with great simplicity. Perhaps people forget how incredibly demanding his standards were. However, if you belong to his school of prayer you'll find inspiration for prayer in God's creation and in the joys and sufferings of his people. Thanksgiving will come readily to your lips, and you'll identify strongly with people in need, praying for them with deep commitment. Your idealism will be hurt by conflicts among God's people and you'll then find inspiration in the reconciling death and abundant new life of Jesus Christ. You will probably be found putting personal action behind your prayers; you get involved, often at great cost to yourself. You find fellow feeling with Luke's Gospel where women, the poor and the sick are especially in evidence.

The important thing about these 'schools of prayer', remember, is that they merely offer you a home base, a place to recognize as your natural preference. They aren't meant to box you in but rather to give you an approximate description of where you feel most comfortable, so that you can go on your way rejoicing, and picking up as many good gifts from other ways of praying as you can. If you know where home is, you can relax.

This journey is for a lifetime. The rucksack is as large as you want, but it's always light. The Guide of guides is at your side. The way is open before you. So the vital thing now is to get moving and to keep moving.

> *If you can't fly, run. If you can't run, walk. If you can't walk, crawl. But by all means – keep moving.*
> *Martin Luther King*

PRAYER

Holy God, compassionate Christ, tender Spirit,
whose love is inexhaustible and whose patience is infinite:
take us and shape us we pray
by the persuasive power of your love,
and as we hold out against your gracious hand,
still smile forgiveness upon our folly,
and love us into strong and willing surrender,
that we may be yours
and you may be ours
and our lives reflect the beauty that we see
in Jesus Christ our Lord.

RESOURCES

Books on prayer are produced by the metre. All I do here is suggest a few starting points. There are so many different styles, so when you find a book that really helps you, treasure it!

General

Approaches to Prayer, Henry Morgan (ed.), SPCK, 1991. Full of useful ideas.

Living Prayer, Metropolitan Anthony Bloom, DLT, 1966. (Also *School for Prayer*, DLT, 1970.) Classics from the Eastern tradition but speaking straight to the West.

Prayer, Richard Foster, Hodder and Stoughton, 1992. A solid way into prayer from a popular and clear writer.

Praying Through Life, Stephen Cottrell, National Society/Church House Publishing, 1998. This is a practical and accessible book on how to relate all of life to prayer.

Taste and See, Margaret Silf, DLT, 1999. An accessible introduction to many forms of prayer, particularly ones using the imagination.

Too Busy Not to Pray, Bill Hybels, IVP, 1998. Practical and faith-building.

Books of prayers

A Silence and a Shouting, Eddie Askew, The Leprosy Mission, 2001 (and various titles by the same author). Popular meditations out of everyday experience and biblical passages.

All Desires Known, Janet Morley, SPCK, 1992. Imaginative, evocative images often with a haunting beauty.

An Anglican Companion, Alan Wilkinson and Christopher Cocksworth (eds), SPCK, 2001. Some of the classic prayers and sources of Anglican spirituality.

The Book of a Thousand Prayers, Angela Ashwin, Marshall Pickering, 1996. An excellent anthology of old and new, including many of the editor's own poetic prayers.

Bread of Tomorrow, Janet Morley (ed.), SPCK, 1992. Prayers from the world Church with a rich variety of cultural styles.

Just As I Am, Ruth Etchells, Triangle, 1994. A rich companion of personal prayers to make your own at the beginning and end of the day.

The Lion Prayer Collection, Mary Batchelor (ed.), Lion, 1996. Another beautifully produced and comprehensive book of prayers in different styles.

Pocket Prayers, Christopher Herbert (ed.), National Society/Church

House Publishing, 1993. Full of classic prayers which have stood the test of time.

Prayers to Remember, Colin Podmore (ed.), DLT, 2001. As it says – some of the best.

The SPCK Book of Christian Prayer, SPCK, 1995. An imaginative, reliable and comprehensive collection of prayers from different Christian traditions.

Tides and Seasons, David Adam, Triangle, 1989. One of the writer's excellent books drawing on the Celtic tradition of prayer. See also *The Open Gate*, Triangle, 1994.

Intercession

The Intercessions Handbook, John Pritchard, SPCK, 1997. Creative ideas for public prayer, prayer groups and personal prayer.

Prayers for All Seasons, Books 1 and 2, Nick Fawcett, Kevin Mayhew, 2000. Three hundred contemporary prayers for all sorts of situations.

Prayers of Intercession, Susan Sayers, Kevin Mayhew, 2000. Intended mainly for public worship.

Prayer and personality

Three books among many which explore the fertile relationship between our personalities and how we prefer to pray.

Knowing Me, Knowing You, Malcolm Goldsmith and Martin Wharton, SPCK, 1993.

Personality and Prayer, Ruth Fowke, Eagle, 1997.

Pray Your Way, Bruce Duncan, DLT, 1993.

Meditation and the use of silence

Both Alike to Thee, Melvyn Matthews, SPCK, 2000. Explores mysticism as a key part of our spiritual journey, discovering God in all things.

Contemplative Prayer, Thomas Merton, DLT, 1973; also *Thoughts in Solitude*, Burns and Oates, 1958. Two of many spiritual classics from a great American monk/writer.

Letters from the Desert, Carlo Carretto, DLT, 1972. Another contemporary classic on the spiritual life.

Open to God, Joyce Huggett, Hodder and Stoughton, 1989. This book opens up traditional methods of meditation in fresh ways.

Sadhana: A Way to God, Anthony de Mello, Doubleday/Image, 1984. Christian exercises in meditation and silence using both western and eastern forms.

This Sunrise of Wonder, Michael Mayne, Fount, 1995. An inventory of joy, leading us to re-examine the importance of wonder in our lives.

The Word is Very Near You: A Guide to Praying with Scripture, Martin L. Smith, Cowley Publications, 1989. Just what it says.

Prayer and social change

God of Surprises, Gerard Hughes, DLT, 1985. Links the inner journey with the needs of a just society to produce one of the great contemporary books of spiritual guidance.

His Love is a Fire, Brother Roger of Taizé, Geoffrey Chapman Mowbray, 1990. Together with other books from Taizé, this book of key writings links personal and social change.

Praying the Kingdom, Charles Elliott, DLT, 1985. An award-winning book which develops a political spirituality for ordinary Christians.

Sharing the Darkness, Sheila Cassidy, DLT, 1988. About the nature and cost of Christian discipleship in the front line of caring.

A Wee Worship Book, Wild Goose Worship Group, Wild Goose Publications, 1999. All writings from Iona have the inner and outer journeys in imaginative partnership.

Classics

Be Still and Know, Michael Ramsey, Collins Fount, 1982.

The Cloud of Unknowing, Penguin, 1961.

Confessions, St Augustine, Penguin, 1961.

The Imitation of Christ, Thomas à Kempis, Collins Fount, 1963.

The Practice of the Presence of God, Brother Lawrence, Hodder and Stoughton, 1989.

Revelations of Divine Love, Julian of Norwich, Penguin, 1966.

The Sacrament of the Present Moment, Jean-Pierre de Caussade, Collins Fount, 1981.

Structured forms of prayer and Bible reading

Beginning Again, John Pritchard, SPCK, 2000, pp. 22–3, 'One to One'; among a variety of (structured and less structured) ways of praying.

Beyond Words, Patrick Woodhouse, Kevin Mayhew, 2001. A rich contemplative shape for daily prayer.

Celebrating Common Prayer (pocket version), Society of St Francis, Mowbray, 1994. A rich form of daily prayer, easier to use in the abridged version.

Celtic Daily Prayer: A Northumbrian Office, The Northumbria Community, Marshall Pickering, 1994.

Woven into Prayer, Angela Ashwin, Canterbury Press, 1999. Contains a thread for the day, a form of daily prayer, a quiet space and a night blessing, throughout the year.

Bible Reading Fellowship (BRF), Peter's Way, Sandy Lane West, Oxford OX4 5HG, produces a variety of schemes for regular Bible reading.

Scripture Union, 207 Queensway, Bletchley, Milton Keynes MK2 2EB, produces another well-established range of notes for all ages.

Theology

Does God Answer Prayer?, Peter Baelz, DLT, 1982. Goes deeper than the normal question of whether prayer 'works'.

Perspectives on Prayer, Fraser Watts (ed.), SPCK, 2001. Perspectives from the Bible, science, psychology, poetry, music, sexuality, etc.

Science and Providence, John Polkinghorne, SPCK, 1989. Sections on prayer in this and other writings from this eminent scientist/priest.

True Prayer, Kenneth Leech, Sheldon Press, 1980. A well-established introduction to the life of prayer and the Christian spiritual tradition.

The Use of Prayer, Neville Ward, Epworth, 1967. Wise, thoughtful and practical.

Websites

Sacred Space on www.jesuit.ie/prayer offers daily prayer online, which sensitively leads the visitor from a way of preparing the body for prayer through to meditation on a Bible passage.

www.ship-of-fools.com is subtitled 'the magazine of Christian unrest'. It has a mass of interesting and offbeat material, including some of spiritual and prayerful interest.